DEAR STRANGER, I KNOW HOW YOU FEEL

Also by Ashish Bagrecha

Dear Stranger, You Deserve to be Loved

Love, Hope and Magic

A JOURNEY TO LOVE AND HEALING

DEAR STRANGER, I KNOW HOW YOU FEEL

ASHISH BAGRECHA

HarperCollins *Publishers* India

First published in 2019

This edition published in India by HarperCollins *Publishers* in 2022
4th Floor, Tower A, Building No. 10, Phase II, DLF Cyber City,
Gurugram, Haryana – 122002
www.harpercollins.co.in

2 4 6 8 10 9 7 5 3 1

P-ISBN: 978-93-5629-337-3
E-ISBN: 978-93-5629-341-0

Typeset by SÜRYA, New Delhi

Printed and bound at
Thomson Press (India) Ltd

For all the strangers fighting the dark days.
I'll always write about you, for you, to you.

the truth is
you are at war with yourself
that's why
you find yourself at war with others.

CONTENTS

PREFACE

I want to thank you for choosing to read this book. It is a passionate expression of my love and understanding for you and everything that you are going through. Thank you for giving me this chance, dear stranger. I hope I can help you in one way or another.

I don't know much about you. I don't know where you live, what you do for a living, whether you study or work, whether you are healthy or poorly, whether you have children or are still a child yourself. I do know that you are feeling lost. A feeling I am all too familiar with myself. I don't know the details of your life, and you don't know mine, but I want you to know you are not alone in your feelings. I might not know or understand exactly why you are feeling lost, but I hope you can trust me when I say that I have been there. I have experienced what you are going through, and I need you to know that I understand.

And that is why I am writing these letters to you: to let you know that you are not alone, and that you are understood. Your feelings are understood. No matter how difficult life feels and how dark it sometimes looks, there is still hope and there is still light, and you are still cared for. The universe cares about you. Your loved ones care about you. I care about you.

I have been on the other side of the light and I know how dark it can sometimes feel. I have experienced the hurt and the low spirits. I have felt the pain and the loneliness. I just wish that, when I had felt like that, someone had written me a letter to help me see I am not alone. There was no one, but I want to be that person for you. I have realised that most of us struggle with our mental health as we experience life's lessons and battles, but there is always someone else who is going through something similar. It might not be the same struggle, but the pain can be very like yours. I hope that with these letters, you can see that you are not alone in your pain and that there are ways to overcome your feelings. It is okay that you can't see them yet, but you will.

Writing these letters has given me the opportunity to share my experience with you. Try to read at least one letter every day, and I hope you can begin to find comfort in your time of need. I hope this will help you to open up a conversation with your loved ones or to write down your own experiences and feelings. There are so many ways to express ourselves— choose something that makes you comfortable. Don't give up hope yet. I hope these letters can help you to work on healing yourself or even to ask for the support you need. It is out there, I promise. Don't give up.

DAY 1

in the deep black sky
even though a million miles apart
the sun still finds a way
to bring light to the moon,

and you expect me
to leave you in this darkness?

ABOUT PAIN

Dear Stranger,

I see you trying hard to cover up your pain, to pretend it doesn't hurt to breathe. That, with every beat of your heart, your chest aches and tears burn deep down in your throat. It doesn't matter if you saw it coming or not; it hurts. The pain feels so deep, so primal, that you don't know if you will survive it. I understand that emotional pain hurts as deeply as physical pain, and I know you are trying to make it through this swamp of icy-cold fear. This fear threatens to shut you down forever and the pain threatens to drown you. I see you trying to control the pain, gasping for air, drowning in this pool of despair, but I also see you far too comfortable being alone, suffering through this.

You are drowning, drowning in emotion, drowning in a tide of what you feel you cannot control. I know you understand that peace is on the shore and that the shore is within reach, but like those drifting out to sea, those who are consumed in the moment, you are panicking. Terrified that you will never breathe again, that you will be dragged under once again, and some invisible force will take hold of you and pull you out so deep that the shore will no longer be an option. I understand the emotions and feelings that are causing you pain are like waves washing over you. They pull you under, overwhelm you, tire you out until you feel nothing but exhaustion. I see you with the lifebuoy in your hand, your will to live slowly extinguishing while you decide whether floating in this sea of pain will be easier than the effort it will take to get you to shore. I am waiting there for you with a blanket of love to wrap you in tightly. I am with you even when you finally decide that the comfort of the shore requires too much effort. When you choose to hold on to your pain, not realising that it is the one thing that both keeps you afloat and threatens to eventually drown you.

I see you suspended in your loneliness, choosing to wallow in your pain rather than swim to shore. Your friends call out to you from the shore; they reassure you that you do not need to face the pain alone anymore. And I see you turn your back on them, crying in shame, deeply uncomfortable with what is happening. I know that you fear both the safety of their support and the comfort of being alone. I see the tears flow down your cheeks but you have become so used to the pain that you fear no longer feeling it. Your eyes beseech me; they ask why I do not swim out to you, why I do not ease your pain and help you through your exhaustion while I guide you to the shore. The thing is, I know that you shouldn't go into the water with someone who is drowning. Your sheer panic and desperate need to be saved may drown both of us while I seek to pull you ashore. So I have thrown you the lifebuoy, dear stranger, and I am here, comforter in hand.

Right now, you need to start kicking, not to keep afloat, but to propel yourself to the shore. I will be here, helping to pull you in. I will listen to your cries of pain and I will weep with you, but together, we will find solutions and you will keep swimming to shore. I will call out instructions: Stop swimming, put your feet down. You are waist-deep, almost there. Keep talking to me and I will help you find the positives, the reasons you should allow yourself to be healed. Keep wading through the pain; knee-deep now, you are almost there. I am here, affirming that your pain is real but helping you find incentives to keep moving towards the shore. Ankle-deep, you no longer need the lifebuoy. Let go of that which caused you this horrible, intense pain, and allow it to drift back out to sea without you. Keep your eyes on me; don't look back. Remember the pain but do not allow it to take you back in. Find comfort in me and in your friends.

I will wrap my blanket of positive affirmations around you and together we will create warmth. Together we can acknowledge your pain but affirm that there are solutions. I will encourage you to write down all the things that are causing you pain and help you find peace. But first you must acknowledge that although the negative emotions were not caused by you, staying adrift in an ocean of pain was your choice because you were comfortable there, and that you understand you can never be comfortable in your pain again.

Know that if you ever find yourself drifting out, away from the shore again, I will be here for you. And when you are safe and no longer drowning, I will be here to help you recover. To help restore your positive energy and pull you through this so that one day you may also help others who are drowning. All you have to do, dear stranger, is start. Kick. Swim to shore. I am waiting for you. I will help you; just start.

Your new beginning awaits.

DAY 2

maybe you'll never know
why i never said a word
why i pushed you away
why i buried my feelings
why i chained my heart
and hid its key
under the deepest sea

because i couldn't allow you to drown
in the never-ending chaos
which was only mine.

ABOUT EMPTINESS

Dear Stranger,

I know that you are feeling empty and alone. I know that your mind threatens to shut your heart out and that you feel as if your soul left you a long time ago. I may not know the exact reasons why, but I do know that the feeling is eating you up inside. I see you slowly abandoning who you are, trying to gain the approval of others. I need you to know that perfection is not necessary. That your flaws make you unique and wonderful. I know that the feeling of emptiness inside you is a vacuum that threatens to consume every other emotion that you used to feel. When you wake in the morning and you are forced to continue with the day's routines, I understand that you feel like an observer. As if you are watching somebody else's life. And you wonder. Wonder how you became so detached from your body and so entangled in your own mind. They tell you that you are emotionless, but the truth is, you feel too intensely. It is never enough. It is always too much. Too much noise, too much pain, just too much.

It is so difficult to explain how you can be so emotional and yet devoid of emotion at the same time. The problem is that none of the emotions that brought happiness or comfort in solitude are within your reach anymore. Instead, your feelings overwhelm you; you feel uncomfortable, unfulfilled and confused. The place where your heart once was, where butterflies and excitement once resided, is now hollow. What you thought was your purpose in life now seems pointless. A sense of failure occupies the place where ambition and hope once lived. What you once dreamed of now feels like a perpetual nightmare, a continuous spiral of negativity and despair.

They tell you to reach out, to speak to people who can guide you to the meaning of life, who can heal you. But you know. You know that people often disappoint you, that it seems as though they never have enough time for you. Or worse. You feel like a burden. When you tried to seek help from someone, you felt as if you were listening in on a conversation that was not meant for you. The shame and guilt burned deep inside, and so you never went back.

I understand that you are tired. Tired of never being strong enough, or beautiful enough, of always feeling second-best. No, not even that. Of feeling like you're not even an option. You guard your heart and build walls around your mind. It is better to keep others out. Out of this pit of darkness that consumes you, I see you emerge to enter the crowd, smiling, participating, pretending that you fit in. I know that that is not how you feel. That you are smiling because it is what is expected of you. That the void is bottomless and that being here with these people only makes you feel lonelier. You don't relate, you do not want to relate to these people. They do not understand you. How could they? How could anyone? And so, when you go home at night, the void begins to consume you again.

Desolation. That is all there is, desolation. No joy, no happiness. Nothing can satisfy you. I see you reaching for your phone, scrolling mindlessly, searching for something that will make you feel less alone in that moment. Perhaps you have immersed yourself in your work. Look how successful you are, they all say. If only they knew that you work to fill the void. You feel as if you have lost your soul. You wonder if it will wander aimlessly forever, or if one day it might find its way back to you.

Dear stranger, I want you to know that you do not need to live this way forever. You are the master of your own existence, and you have the power to turn your life around. I want you to know that the void can be filled, and that although it threatens to devour you right now, it will not if you do not allow it to. Your soul is not lost; it is hiding, inside you. Like a small scared child, it has chosen to protect itself in the deepest recesses of your psyche. It wants you to find it and return it to its rightful place. When you practise meditation, when you are mindful and aware once again, you will reconnect with your soul.

Please pursue fulfilment relentlessly. Explore and chase with vigour what sets your soul on fire. Set goals, meet them, and celebrate your success. Allow yourself to feel. Feel all of it. The anger, the despair, the hurt and the pain. Feel them with ferocity and then channel them into something constructive. Some of the greatest works of art have been born out of an acute feeling of emptiness. You cannot cure your feelings; you simply need to feel them to come through to the other side. Reach out. You are not a burden. Although I know that you feel disconnected right now, those who love you will continue to help you fill the void while you learn how to do it yourself.

Love yourself with all your heart. You may not feel like you are the most important person in the lives of others, but you are always number one to yourself. Take care of yourself; be gentle and don't criticise yourself. You have a purpose; you would not have been created if you did not. So, love yourself for the purpose you have not yet found. Understand that some people live their whole lives without knowing what their purpose is, but find happiness and joy in the pursuit of their purpose. And finally, dear stranger, please don't punish yourself. I promise that nothing other than love and patience can heal the void inside. Punishing yourself will only feed the darkness. Remember that the moon and the stars need the darkness in order to shine. Shine, dear stranger, shine. Every day will feel warmer and lighter once you begin learning how to shine for yourself.

Sending you comfort and acceptance.

DAY 3

my dear demons
no matter how many times
you try to prove
that nobody loves me,
you'll always fail!

i'm loved
and I know that;
i suggest you run
and never come back!

ABOUT ANXIETY

Dear Stranger,

I see you in the corner of the room—avoiding eye contact with everyone, hoping to fade into the background and prevent any real attention from coming your way. I hear your anxious cries of 'no, no, no' through torturous social rituals like being sung to on your birthday. I understand your need to shrink into a ball so small that not even a cat would notice you as something to play with and torment. I feel your thoughts crowding your head as rooms grow louder. I see that you are suffering. Suffering alone is the most painful place to be, and suffering in silence feels like torture. Try to remember that you are not alone, that I see you.

I promise that you are not alone in feeling that your anxious monster takes up more space in every room than you can fathom. I understand he mocks and teases and tortures you throughout the day, and does not get even remotely tired in the evening. In fact, in the evening, he is worse. At night, he's as energetic as a child after eating loads of sweets on Diwali or Halloween. He stomps around, throwing tantrums and shouting through your evenings as you lie awake watching the sky change colour, and as the sun sets and rises yet again. What happens if you never sleep again, you often ask yourself. What really can happen? I don't know, but it can't hurt to try and drift off. It's got to be better than not trying at all.

Yes, I know, that fatal word. *Try.* You hear it daily when you need to leave the house, or get dressed, or take a shower, and your anxiety wins yet another battle. Why don't you try and get out of bed today? Try. I know you do. I know you try your hardest every day to summon the energy you need to fight this evil beast. I know you try to ignore the panic that rushes through your bloodstream at the mere mention of going to a public place. I know you try to calm your heartbeat every time you step over the threshold of your front door and out into the real world. I know you squeeze your hands together every time you find yourself nervously tapping your feet. I know you try to still the flurry of thoughts that come with every opportunity, bringing more panic and dread. I know the angst that comes with considering a social engagement and the added pressure of your monster trying to provoke you into avoidance. I know.

No matter how much your monster mocks you and says that nobody understands, they do. And I don't mean everyone. Some people are indifferent to their anxious monsters. Some people don't have to battle a panic that overcomes their bodies every day. They don't worry about all the potential hazards they might face if they leave the house. They don't perceive social activities as painful events. Instead they see them as what they should be—time to unwind and have fun. Your time to unwind, on the other hand, looks more like hiding from the world.

But there are many of us out there who do understand how it feels to confront your anxious monster every single day. Remember, you are not alone with him. There is a community of people like us who are now shouting back at our monsters to quieten their roars. Once upon a time, like you, many in our community didn't feel like they had a voice to shout back. It will change for you, just like it has for us. You will find that inner strength you've been hiding, to fight back. You will grow louder and begin to feel you're in charge again one day. Your monster will grow smaller and weaker as a result. In the meantime, just keep trying. Yes, try.

And don't worry, today I will go to the shop to get your milk for you. Tomorrow though, maybe we could try and go together? And then, maybe next week, you could try and go on your own? Or not, it is totally your call. I will not push you because I know it will only increase your stress and panic. I am here for you, to be by your side or to lend an ear, whenever you need me. If that is every day or even every waking moment, I am here. Life may throw you a few curveballs even as you find your feet, but I will be there to support you and lift you up when they knock you off balance. Which they will, because that is life after all: an unending series of challenges we must face and fight against for happiness and, sometimes, sanity.

I know it feels easier to hide away when anxiety has the stronger hand, but if you reach out you will find others who will help you to face it all. With support, your hand grows stronger and your opponent weakens. You are kind and loved. You are generous and caring. You are not frail, no matter how weak you feel. You are strong and you are brave. You are stronger and braver than your anxious monster. Don't let him win.

You may not see it now, but I can see it. Even your anxious monster can see your true potential and he shouts and barks at you just to hold on to his power, because he knows all you need to overrule him is to see it in yourself. I can see that fire in your stomach burning low, but still burning. I can see that switch in your brain awaiting power. It sits there, dormant for now, but it can be flipped at any moment. While you cannot see the light at the end of this very dark tunnel, I can see it. Only a few feet ahead of you, the clearing will come into view. Don't try to walk any faster; it's okay. Go at your own pace along the journey, and soon enough, you will see the light too.

Reach out and hold my hand; I'll help you through the darkness. Reach out and understand that I have felt your suffering. Reach out and find a hand, waiting to support you through it all. Reach out.

And when you reach out, don't expect that miracle switch to flip all of a sudden. Take it easy and be patient with yourself, stranger. Take each day as another opportunity to make your way towards that light.

Sending you love and light, today and every day.

DAY 4

the moon reminds me of you
how beautifully you both try
to fight the darkness.

ABOUT INSOMNIA

Dear Stranger,

I just wanted to say that I see you dragging yourself through the days and nights with difficulty. I see your exhaustion as you try and manage daily life, gripping on to sanity as best you can. I see you yawning at your desk every five minutes, sipping on your fourth cup of coffee of the morning. I see you staring vacantly into space as the demons run riot inside your head, never allowing you a moment of peace. I see you fall asleep on the bus, waking up in a blind panic as the demons in your head scream at you. I see your dread as the day draws to a close and you realise that another sleepless night is on the horizon.

Stranger, the chaos and constant whirlwind of your thoughts are not just yours. I have my demons too. Sometimes, I sit in my room and allow my demons to have a party, giving them only an hour or so to run riot before they *must* head to bed. Don't allow the party to go on into the early hours; you need your beauty sleep after all. Let them celebrate and rage and drink too much and dance too hard, but don't let it go past *your* curfew. Remind your demons that you are boss.

When you put your head on your pillow at night, tell those demons to turn out the lights too. Don't allow them to smash and crash and burn down everything you love. Don't let them rob you. Sometimes, I bet you wish the demons were physical beings so you could smash and crash and burn them down. I bet you wish you could call the police to shut the party down and send everyone home. But the police can't stop this chaos; only you have that power. Sometimes, reaching out for help is the best thing you can do.

Don't let your demons rob you of your dreams, taunting you as you watch the sun set and then rise again, desperate for just a few moments of peace. I hear your cries in the night as the despair kicks in. I hear your sleepless stirring on your bed. I hear you, exasperated and pacing in the hallway so as to not wake up your loved ones. I hear you moving from room to room in your home in the hope that a change of location will help you find peace. I hear you all night, rummaging around the house, looking in cupboards, trying out herbal remedies you have looked up on the internet.

The only time I don't hear you, poor stranger, is in the daytime.

In the daytime, you fight through every minute and every hour with grace and strength. You drag your feet hopefully through the day, saving as much energy as you can for the battle of the evening. You conserve the energy to communicate because you know your demons will zap it all away soon enough. You caffeinate and fill your body with carbohydrates in an attempt to store some form of energy. You may find yourself going outdoors to 'blow away the cobwebs', but don't allow them to blow you away too.

I hear you every evening as you take a deep breath and reach for the handle of your bedroom door. Your insomnia and your demons wait like excited children, ready to tell you everything you have missed whilst you have been away. Not that you really get the chance to 'be away' from them. Regardless, your sleeplessness bounces eagerly like a puppy who craves attention. It yaps and leaps and runs in circles in your bedroom. Your demons play happily on your bed, jumping up and down like in a bouncy castle, waiting for you to arrive at the party. You put on your diffuser, filling the space with the smell of lavender; maybe the calm scent will make them leave. You put on your sleep lamp with its softening colour;

maybe the absence of strobe lights will make them leave. You put on your meditation app; maybe, if you ignore them long enough, it will make them leave. You play the sounds of waves and rain, filling your bedroom with sounds of the outdoors; maybe the lack of rave music will make them leave. Anything to make them leave.

Your body heating up under your duvet, you throw it off only to find you've been holding yourself tight for safety. You replace the duvet with a blanket; maybe that will help cool you down. No, too cold now, so you switch back to the duvet. Listen to me: open your window, and let the smells of nature and the night breeze fill your bedroom. Whatever you do, ignore the sounds of traffic. Don't listen to the drunken pedestrians making their way home. Don't think about every night out you have ever had in detail. Switch off your brain. Party's over in your bedroom. Enforce the curfew.

It isn't fair for you to have to work so hard for a good night's sleep, though. You shouldn't have to fight through the day and make constant changes to improve your evenings. Reach out and ask for support; there are probably methods you haven't tried yet that a health professional could suggest. Try everything you can, sleepless stranger. Try exercising to tire yourself out, try vitamins, try counselling, try herbal teas before bed, try banning screen time in your room, try reading instead of watching TV, try meditation, try essential oils, try talking to a friend, try everything. One day, you will lay your head on your pillow and find that the anxiety about sleep has dissipated, or at least eased off.

If you reach out and discuss your problems, letting your demons have the microphone for a while, you may find they leave you in peace in the evenings. Spend a bit of time interacting with them; don't ignore them entirely. Just like a child or a puppy, your demons need to be played with. Take them out with you on a walk in the evening; let them have the floor to moan about life for a while. Then, tell them you will see them tomorrow, and go your separate ways. Don't let the party continue back at yours.

I hear your sleepless pacing. I hear your anxiety build as the evening draws in. I hear your tired yawns all day. Time to make yourself heard, stranger. Take each day as another opportunity to talk about your difficulties and you will find the next day gets easier. Healing is not a race, but a long voyage that you must embark on.

Sending you peaceful dreams and calming energy.

DAY 5

you weren't born with a heartbreak,
you won't die with one,
then why live with it?

this world has so much to offer,
you deserve better.

accept, allow.
embrace, evolve.

ABOUT HEARTACHE

Dear Stranger,

I know that it feels like your world is crashing down right now and the only time you feel like getting out of bed is when you need to fetch another box of tissues. I know that it feels like your soul will crack when those closest to you tell you that you're overreacting, that it is not that bad, or that the overwhelming sadness will not last forever. I see you lying in bed at night, distraught, inconsolable, unable to breathe because the pain in your chest is too much to bear. I understand that heartbreak is as physical as it is emotional. I know it hurts. Don't listen to them. Don't listen to those who tell you to compartmentalise your pain. Your loss is real, your pain is real, and your heart is broken.

I have been where you are, crouched in a corner on your knees, rocking yourself, trying desperately to soothe yourself the way you did when you were a child. Your eyes are swollen. Even your tears cause you pain; they burn your skin as they roll down your cheeks. Your nose is raw and your head pounds—not just physical pain, but an emotional ache that will not let up. It will not let you be. Sick. You feel sick. Your stomach churns as broken thoughts fight wildly in your mind. They claw at your psyche, begging to be let free, in the same way that the sick claws its way up your throat, wanting to be violently expelled from your body. Your ears ring. You want to scream but it won't come out. You are sure that, if you did, the sound would be unfamiliar. When you talk, it is not your voice that leaves your mouth, but the voice of a stranger. A person filled with pain and suffering. A person you wished you didn't know. I have been where you are.

I understand that you have no control over how you feel right now. I too told myself that there was a time frame for this pain. That my heart should be healed by now because that is what everyone was telling me. I know what they're saying: ten days is all it takes to heal a broken heart. I cannot tell you why yours still feels broken. Why your heart races so fast that it feels like it may burst from your chest so as to leave this broken human being and search for sanctuary in someone who understands that the mind controls pain and that feelings can be rationalised. I know what it is like to move through each day with a painted face, like a puppet on a string. Your movements are not your own: they belong to the puppet master, the loved ones expecting to see healing.

They say you are coping well, yet you look tired. You should get some sleep. But sleep is for those whose hearts are whole. Your sleep gives way to hours of ceiling-staring, as thoughts race wildly through your head. The what-ifs, the could-have-beens. When you close your eyes, you are haunted by memories. Memories that once used to bring you joy now bring only pain. You toss, turn, watch the clock. Eventually, you revert to old photos to reminisce, to force your mind to remember a time when you felt joy, or anything but this searing pain.

I remember when they would tell me to eat. Eat? Did they not know that my stomach was in a perpetual knot? Anxiety gripped me so tight that it felt like it may suffocate me until the last dregs of light had left my soul. Besides, I was eating. Eating enough to ensure that I did not pass out, but not enough to make me feel full. Fullness brought nausea with it and I was so tired of feeling ill. So I know that you feel physically ill. You are sure that fate has played a cruel trick on you. As if your heartbreak was not enough, you now have to deal with illness as well. You feel run down and feverish. Your skin crawls. Your stomach burns, and you are not sure if it is from the permanent hollowness inside you or if there is something seriously wrong with your health.

I used to tell myself that I had turned into a hypochondriac. Recurrent feelings of illness and thoughts of mortality had me constantly questioning my sanity. I know what it is like to try so hard to feel normal, when the feeling of emptiness won't leave you in peace. I know that you feel hollow, and that you do not understand how you can feel so empty and yet feel so much pain. It feels as if your life has become a tragic comedy of opposites and contradictions. You feel like you are drowning. Drowning in tragedy, drowning in helplessness. And like those who are drowning, you should reach out. Reach out to those who love you. To those who want to ease your pain. Be honest with them and let them know that you are not coping. That ten days is not enough to heal a broken heart. Let them hold your hand and listen to what you have to say. Speak. Speak freely and openly. Allow yourself to feel. Let the feelings overtake you. Do not hold them back, ride on them, and understand that like an ocean current, they will eventually wash you ashore.

Take time to heal your broken heart in whatever way you need to. Eat. Eat enough to keep the nausea at bay. Permit yourself to have fun. Pain is often healed by things that soothe our souls. Allow yourself to remember the good times and understand that, eventually, those memories will no longer cause you pain. I promise you that clarity will come. It may not come quickly, but it will one day, and you will sleep again. One day, the pain in your chest will cease to be. Your stomach will no longer burn and your tears will be controllable once more. But for now, while you are drowning, reach out. Reach out, and your heart will begin to mend one day at a time.

From a fellow broken-hearted soul.

DAY 6

i can't find anyone like you
not even close to you
i look for you in everyone
but i fail every single time
yet i don't feel lonely or sad
i feel happy and proud
the departure doesn't hurt
because i loved the best one.

ABOUT LOSS

Dear Stranger,

Dealing with loss is never easy. I need you to know that there is no right or wrong way to grieve. Your suffering is a natural process, and even though there are days when you feel that it is impossible to carry on without the ones you have lost, you will. Your loss, your grief, is your own. It is entirely personal. I know that it is all-consuming at times, that you wish sometimes that you could shove your emotions into the deepest recesses of your mind and lock them away. But you won't survive like that. Like a pent-up wild animal, it will push through and continue to torment you until you face it head on.

There will be days where your anger will boil inside, threatening to explode. When you will feel the need to fall to your knees and scream until you have no air left in your lungs to power your voice. Do it. Scream until you can't scream anymore. It doesn't matter what anybody thinks. I know that you feel alone, and that no one understands. The truth is, no one really does. You will grow tired of people and their advice, and that is okay. I understand why being told to be strong does nothing but fuel your wrath.

Be strong, they say. For what? For whom? Is grief not allowed when you have experienced a loss? There is no need to be strong. There is no need to suppress your pain. You are entitled to the questions that fill your head. The whys and hows are natural. Don't let anyone tell you otherwise. But please know this: it isn't your fault. There was nothing you could have done. You have the right to ask questions and you have the right to fall apart. You don't owe anyone an explanation when you are alone at night and your grief overtakes you. I see you, curled into a ball, begging for answers. Pleading for the feeling of emptiness to be replaced with something, anything other than despair.

You are not weak. You are not the negative words you keep repeating to yourself. You are human, and your pain is relevant. They told you to spend time with friends, to meet new people who will not remind you of your life before the pain. They encourage you to be 'normal', to move on. Move on? How do you move on from something that was part of your life? I know you do not want to move on, not now, not any time in the near future. I know that you do not want to forget. The thought of forgetting is so painful that it knocks the breath from your lungs and threatens to rip your soul in two. I can hear you begging, bargaining for one more moment. One more experience, one more hug or kiss or a chance to hear their voice, just once more. You don't understand why your life has been so unfairly, irrevocably, changed.

Today, you thought you were doing better until someone reminded you that it was an important date. You have tried to forget these days, in order to find clarity. And you thought you had improved, that the wound was no longer raw. But it will resurface when you're least expecting it, and you will be caught in a tidal wave of pain yet again. I can see you trying to justify the time it has taken for you to grieve. Please stop. Loss is permanent; your feelings will be permanent. There will be days when you are able to cope, and there will be days when you will not. The truth is, you will learn to become accustomed to the hole in your heart. It will never go away, but as you heal and teach yourself how to cope, it will get better. Your mind will heal and your heart will hurt a little less. The ache of loneliness and grief will fade, and the hole will begin to feel like it was always there.

I can see you roll your eyes in frustration when you are told that it will get better. I promise you, it will. It might not look like your idea of 'better', but there will be an improvement. Anger and backward steps will give way to acceptance and peace. You will learn to live again. You will be different. You will have changed, and that is okay.

Reach out to friends, to family, to anyone who will listen without judgement. Having a shoulder to cry on is invaluable. I know that you feel completely alone in this, but you aren't. Remember that not everyone grieves in the same way. The tears may not come, or they may come much later. Just because you have not cried, it does not mean that you did not care. There is no shame in seeking help from a professional counsellor if you feel it is all too much. Therapists and grief counsellors have spent years studying and practising, specifically to help people who are going through what you are going through. They can teach you how to work through the intense feelings that are causing you so much turmoil. I know that you just don't want to try right now. But even if you have lost all interest in self-care, take care of yourself. Be gentle and non-critical. I understand that you are your own biggest critic, but being critical of yourself in your time of loss will only make you feel lousier than you already do.

Emotional pain, like a physical injury, takes time to heal. Make time for yourself; do something you enjoy.

Join a gym or take up yoga. You cannot heal a festering wound if you refuse to administer the correct treatment. Understand that facing your feelings head-on will equip you with the tools to learn to live with your loss. Allow yourself to feel, to really feel all of it—the loss, the pain, the grief, the anger. Feeling it all is the best remedy you could opt for.

And finally, when it all feels like it's too much, hold on. Hold on tight. It will pass. I promise you: one day you will wake up and it will be better. You will feel better. You will come out of this a little scarred and a little bruised, but you will come through. Each day, the wound will hurt a little less than the day before.

Please. Just hold on.

From a concerned friend.

DAY 7

that storm in your heart
let it thunder
let it strike
let it rain
let it flood
let it destroy
let it destruct
and in the aftermath
you will find sunshine
you will find a new life
the storm will cease
and you will find peace.

ABOUT NEGATIVITY

Dear Stranger,

I hear your thoughts: they swirl uncontrollably, like a destructive tornado of negativity. They spew debris upon toxic debris. They hasten to convince you that you are not good enough. Your thoughts spiral out of control, taking over in your most lonely moments. Negativity reigns inside your head; it speaks to you in the darkness as you try to close your eyes in the struggle for a decent night's sleep. A low whisper: *worthless, failure, ugly, stupid.* It might be bearable if the tornado only came at night, but that isn't the case. It preoccupies your mind all day, and with every negative thought it convinces you of, it gains momentum and strength— becoming a powerful creature inside your head with the power to override any feelings of joy or impulses of hope that try to creep in.

I see you when you open your eyes in the morning. I know that the second your conscious mind is awake the storm begins, never leaving you a moment of peace to consolidate your thoughts and feelings. It won't be long before it begins to suck in anything positive, only to throw it back out—twisted and skewed into the most vile opinions of yourself. I know that it is painfully difficult even to lift yourself out of bed. That catching a glimpse of yourself in the mirror as you complete your morning ritual is as risky as crossing a busy freeway.

Hunkered down in crowded spaces, you convince yourself that people are staring at you. That it must be because of the way you look, an alien among normal human beings. And the truth is, you have let yourself go. Washing yourself has become less frequent; dressing to feel smart or unique no longer happens. It is too much effort; it draws too much attention from passers-by. Your mind tells you that you are disgusting, and you promise yourself that you will make the effort to at least wash your hair at the end of the day. But you know the truth. By the time the day has played out, you will be too exhausted to care. Your only priority will be to satiate the most basic needs. And then, energy drained and emotionally worn, you will collapse into your unmade bed—telling yourself that if you set your alarm a little earlier the next day, you will have the time to take care of yourself. I know you won't though, dear stranger, and so do you. Negativity and exhaustion take hold of you, pulling you deep down into your mattress, giving you no space to breathe.

The next day does not bring any relief. You sleep through your alarm, exhausted. And waking up in a fog, you rush to meet society's expectations all over again. I see you among your peers, detached, silently asking yourself why they would possibly want to spend any time with you at all. You know that the person they chose to befriend was someone they met a lifetime ago. But now, failure has overtaken you, and that person has disappeared. Yet you play your part. An actor on a stage, you have nothing positive to say, no stories of success that you believe to be true, but you feel you must convince them anyway. They feel like the only thread that ties you to this earthly realm. Your thoughts manage to convince you that they know you are lying. You try hard to squash the doubts they're putting in your head; you tell yourself you know that these people, your people, choose to be here with you.

But your thoughts lie to you, convincing you that they are only here to mock you once you have left, or that some of them feel sorry for you. For the mess you have become. I see you make an excuse to leave early, telling your friends that you need to complete an important project at work tomorrow. On the way home, you fight the thoughts that call you a liar, jeering that there is absolutely no one who would ever entrust you with a task of major importance. You tell yourself that tomorrow will be better.

I know that you have tried your best to turn your negative thoughts into positive ones, only to have them thrown back at you with an excuse justifying why they are not. Anything positive that you have to say about yourself is twisted by your own mind. Eventually, you tell yourself that your ego was unjustifiably bloated, and that those positive thoughts were somehow illusions of grandeur—a privilege that should only be enjoyed by those who deserve it. You do not feel that you are deserving of much. Not of love or adoration, nor compliments for success or physical attractiveness. Those are reserved for the exceptional and the extraordinary, you feel, and although you believed you were that once, long ago, you no longer believe it to be true.

I want you to know that your positive thoughts are true. That the swirling tornado of negativity is the liar. I know that it is exceptionally convincing, but that is its job. To break you down and make you believe the lies it tells you. Today, I will find a positive thought for every negative it spews out, and I will convince you that what I have said is true. Perhaps tomorrow, we could find the positives together.

You may not believe it right now, in the swirling, destructive chaos of your mind, but you have the ability to banish the tornado forever and to rebuild your shattered ego. I will help you take away the power of negativity; I will help you convince yourself once more that you are not the sum of all your failures but rather the total of all that makes you unique. I will love you until you can once again love yourself with the unconditional ferocity of an undying love. Together, we can overcome this depression. Remember, you are not small and insignificant. You have the power to change, and to overcome. Convince yourself with the help of everything that is positive and good in life. Take each day as it comes; take small steps towards overpowering that negative voice in your head.

Sending you an abundance of energy.

DAY 8

you don't want peace
you want the chaos and the storm
to bring you pain and destroy you
you don't want to be found or loved
you want to stay lost and be left alone
but i won't let you.

every time you walk into darkness
i'll stand right next to you
and dare you
to destroy both of us.

ABOUT SELF-HARM

Dear Stranger,

I feel your soul crack. I hear you beg for the pain to leave your body and release your mind. I know what you are going through is too much to bear right now. I see you lying in bed at night, distraught, inconsolable, unable to breathe, because the pain in your chest feels as if it wants to burst. I know that it does not feel natural, that you feel as if any other kind of pain will help to distract you from the ache in your heart and the mess in your head.

I see you crouched in a corner, blade in hand, hesitating just long enough to convince yourself that this needs to be done. You are nauseous from crying and your head pounds from trying to figure out how an emotion can make you feel so helpless. You pick up the blade. Control. At least *this*, you can control. You bring the blade to your wrist and you rip through the skin. You think about the word 'cutting'. But this is not a cut. It is a rip. Cuts are clean; they can be healed with minimal scarring. These marks are permanent; you will hold them, inside and out, for all eternity. This is a rip, a tear in your skin. Not healing but distracting. Blissfully distracting. The blood that comes to the surface is bright red. You are fascinated by it because it proves that you are alive, and the pain is far greater than that which is inside. So, it distracts you. It takes your mind off what has happened to you in the past, and it focuses your attention on what is happening right now. A rip. A tear. You bring the blade back to your arm and tear through your flesh once again. I know the familiar sting on the other side of this, dear stranger. I know how it feels—the guilt, shame and relief all at once. Please reach out; talk to someone you trust. If you feel like you cannot trust anyone close to you, talk to a stranger. Just talking can help you work through your reasons and find new ways to cope.

I see you hiding your fresh wounds underneath baggy clothes and thick wristbands. You hide them because you know other people will make you feel ashamed. When you venture outside, the shame rises and you wish that you could light a cigarette, pour a drink, anything to distract yourself from the onslaught. I see you reach into your purse. I know that you are looking for the familiar comfort of a steel blade or even digging your keys into your fingers to remind yourself that you are alive. You scratch your arms frantically, as if that would ease the thoughts whirring at lightning speed around your head. Your body aches to vomit up your last meal; it yearns to tighten your belt in a cruel grip round your waist. Your mind lets you consider tightening it around your neck when you are alone at home. You shake your head in an attempt to shake off your suicidal thoughts. When the going gets tough, will hurting yourself always be your first port of call? Your panic rises at the thought. I promise you: it won't always be this way. You have a power inside you that you just haven't realised yet. You can get through this. You are stronger than you know, and I am here to help you see it.

I see you fleeing into a pub, hastily ordering the hardest liquor, something you know will numb the pain inside. You don't mind running into people you know; in fact, their company may even be a welcome distraction or an excuse to justify your daytime drinking. I see you sitting at the bar, downing one drink after the next, occasionally pressing a finger into your fresh wounds, if only to remind yourself that you are still alive. You chain-smoke, willing the nicotine to ease the crushing pain in your chest, and once you are sufficiently numb from alcohol and cigarettes and physical pain, you make your way home. Reach out to your friends in these moments; tell them that you can't help but turn to drinking or to drugs in moments of despair. Tell them you want to hurt yourself. Don't suffer in silence. They will listen.

I know you have considered hoarding tablets, that you've counted them at night to see if you have enough yet to die. I know you've tried to die before. I know how it feels to be so desperate to numb the pain that you believe the only way to overcome the feeling is to stop existing. Please hold on. Please tell someone how you are feeling. You are not alone. You are not the only person to have felt so desperate for the misery to end. I know how it feels. I have been there. I promise it will pass. Please hold on. Please reach out to someone you love, or if you worry about their reaction, reach out to a doctor or counsellor. Look for support in your community. Talk about your feelings, about how you have tried to end things. You are not alone. Keep going. Talk to your doctor; maybe they could prescribe some medication to ease the misery slightly. Use it as a crutch to help yourself get back on your feet. You can overcome this. I have been where you are. I promise you, it will get better.

I know that when you walk home, bleary-eyed from crying and dizzy from self-harm, you see those who have been consumed by drugs and think about the blissful state of unawareness they are in. I know you think about joining them. You have tried drugs in the past, in an attempt to soothe your internal aches, but please know this will not make things any better, dear stranger.

I know that you desperately want to survive this, that the feelings of guilt and shame about the harm you inflict on yourself are a cry for help. I want to help distract you from emotional pain, and from the habits you have built up to numb your pain. I want to help you work through your pain, to allow you to feel and release all that is inside you without judgement or advice. I want to stand next to you while you scream to the heavens and let go of all that has caused you pain. I want to help you equip yourself with the right types of distraction, and I want to be there when you are ready to numb the pain. I want you to hold out your hand so I can lead you through this without your ever having to hurt yourself again. Hold my hand. We can heal this hurt together. It won't happen overnight but, together, we can get through this one day at a time.

Sending you strength and solidarity; I know you have got this.

DAY 9

to those who say
this is a generation
of confused minds
lonely hearts
and broken people,

i ask
which one was not?

so don't worry about us,
we too will find our ways
to live, love and heal.

ABOUT IDENTITY

Dear Stranger,

I see you trying to attain perfection, trying to conform to society's standards of what perfection should be. I know that you have morphed and changed so many times that you no longer know who you are. You do not understand anymore who you are supposed to be, or what makes you unique and special. But I see who you really are, and I understand the pressure of keeping up with the demands of the perfect life you expect of yourself. I know that you no longer know what is expected of you because you no longer know what you expect from yourself.

I see you lost and drifting in your fake world—depressed, lonely and scared. I see you lying in bed at night, scrolling through your friends' feeds, jealous and aching for something real. Some real fun, real connections, real friends. You are struggling with your life choices, trying to make a decision, trying desperately to know where you fit in all of this. You are convinced that people expect you to be something you feel you are not. You compare yourself to others and feel that you should be as successful as they are. That you should at least have achieved what they have by now. You lie in bed berating yourself for not knowing where you fit in, tearing your self-esteem to shreds. You had expected life to be different, for this phase to turn out exactly as you had planned, and now you are so lost that without the good opinion of the people you hold in high regard, you feel you are nothing. You feel that you no longer occupy a meaningful place in humanity because you have failed to achieve what you had set out to. And so, you morph and change, hoping that at some point you will find a way to catch up with those you compare yourself to.

I am still here and I want you to know that you matter. That life does not always pan out the way you expected it to. I see you arguing with yourself, trying to convince yourself that there are other ways to achieve your ideal. You struggle with depression, with thoughts of inadequacy, as you spiral out of control. With every step you take to find out who you are, you seem to lose more of yourself. Pain begins to become the driving factor of your quest. The pain becomes so intense, so ever-present, that you begin to block out everything you once cared about. I know that the second your conscious mind is awake, thoughts of inadequacy start to fill your mind, a battle that prolongs itself into a war for the territory of who you once were and who you want to be. Yet all it takes is one small setback, or one minor detail out of place, for you to feel lost yet again. It soon begins to feel like the only forces left to guide you are the vile opinions you have formed of yourself. I know that it is difficult to get up in the morning not knowing what direction to take. That when you are with those you know, or in places where you once fit perfectly, you now feel like an outsider. And so, you wander around aimlessly until the day finally plays out, and then you end it, drained of energy, and emotionally worn.

I know you believe that the opinions of others matter, and you are not completely wrong. Seek the counsel of those who love you. Find the courage to do new things, and if you find you cannot do them alone, I will be there. Spend time with me so that I can tell you what makes you unique, what your strengths are, and where your weaknesses lie. Take what I have said and apply that knowledge constructively. Find something that sets your soul on fire. Then, strive to do your best and have fun doing it. Take the time to reconnect with your values. Understand that life events may change how you handle and react to certain things, but they will never change your core values. If what you are currently doing goes against those values, stop. And if the thought of no longer being accepted as a consequence fills you with anxiety, reach out to me. Actively seek out those who ground you; they will be the source of your joy, the light that guides you through the darkness that surrounds you.

Dear stranger, you may not believe it right now—as you wander aimlessly along life's path, lost and alone—but you do have the ability to find yourself again. You are capable of rebuilding your identity and giving it a completely new form that is also true to who you are. I know that, right now, it feels like you will be lost forever, but I hold the torch that will guide you. I will help you find your core once more, and I will continually remind you that your failure does not mean the end, but rather the beginning of something beautiful. I will love you while you cannot love yourself and I will teach you how to love the new you.

Together, we can forge a path through all obstacles to find your way home. Remember: you are wonderfully and uniquely made, you have the power to change, you have the power to overcome, and you have the power to find yourself again. Convince yourself that everything that is positive and good in life awaits you, and know that I will be there every step of the way as you move forward and work towards learning to love yourself.

Sending you warmth and light.

DAY 10

we're just two people
trapped in love
trying to fix each other
but failing remarkably.

we're just two people
holding on to hope.

ABOUT HOPE

Dear Stranger,

I have been where you are right now—devastated, defeated, not knowing how to change your situation, wondering if your life is even worth changing. I see you lock eyes with yourself in the mirror each morning. I know that your mind is filled with critical thoughts which begin to tell you, from the second you are awake, that this day, today, you will not achieve enough. That you will not accomplish anything that you set out to do. You stare at yourself in the mirror, thinking how long it has been since you last felt you had achieved anything. You struggle to change your thought patterns, to say something positive to yourself. To try and fix your spiralling thoughts into a cognitive pattern, To be mindful and aware that your thoughts have a direct effect on your day. So, you smile, yet the bitterness builds, and the rage wants to be let out. With every passing morning, with every pep talk gone wrong, and with every day that you feel unsuccessful, hope fades.

Do you remember when hope came easily? Back when you were a child, when your hopes were wrapped around things that are of no consequence to you anymore? Now, hope seems to do nothing but disappoint you. I know that the people around you do not understand, but I do. To them, your hopelessness is confusing. They do not understand why you won't just apply for your dream job, eat healthier, or make new friends after discarding the ones who have mistreated you. But I do understand. I understand that when you have no hope you feel nothing is worth the effort. That anything you try will be futile. I see you blaming yourself for not being able to manage your life; I see how it throws you into a bottomless pit of despair. A despair that only serves to add new thoughts of destruction to your day. I know that when you have no hope, your thoughts are so overpowering, so time-consuming and energy-draining, that motivation leaves you completely. That you simply do not have the energy to make the changes necessary to find a path out of the pit you are in.

Fear consumes you. A fear of rejection, of being lonely forever. You are scared, depressed and anxious. You feel that you are stuck in the same situation. Every day a loop, until, eventually, you grow old in this misery. I know that you are afraid to even try because failure will mean that you have to deal with the pain of disappointment.

You don't know if you can handle any more pain. Because I have been there, I know that your despair, your hopelessness, only sets you up for further failure. Your thoughts will become a self-fulfilling prophecy. I know that if you have no hope, you will stop believing in yourself, and this means that you will not find the courage to hope again. To change your internal dialogue.

I know that it is difficult to change, especially when you can no longer hope that things will change for you. I know that motivation takes energy and that you think you have none. I want to help you find a clear path. I will be your beacon of light in this fog, so you may begin your climb out of this pit towards hope. Together, we will create your plan. We will write down each step. These steps will be the foundation of the path you will lay on your journey. Today, I want you to find a role model—someone who once had to overcome adversity, and found the courage to do so. I want you to read their story, immerse yourself in their life, and look for solutions that apply to you. I want you to speak positively to yourself; I will encourage you with supportive messages, so that once again you can rebuild hope. Please reach out to me when you despair, and understand that it is only natural to lose your way from time to time. Perhaps tonight I can cook you dinner, and tomorrow, you can tell me how your day went while you plan your next step? Once your despair dissipates and you find your way back to your path, help others. Understand that healing others often helps restore your self-worth and the sense that you have a purpose in life. When you have a purpose, you will begin to recover your belief in humanity.

Allow me to help you to become mindful. Mindful of your thoughts and how they shape your future. Let me help you change your dialogue with yourself. Today, we will not talk about what you wish to achieve in the course of the day, not yet anyway. First, I will help you to remember all the qualities that make you unique. I will help you to squash the negativity that rears its head and fights you each morning. If you let me, I will teach you how to love yourself again. I want you to know that hopelessness is not permanent. That if you try, if you allow me to help you, if you regain focus and attention, hope will find you again. That you will find the strength to hope with all your heart, and the ability to achieve anything you set your mind to.

Let's begin our learning process immediately so we can help one another to heal while negotiating life's difficult terrain. Together we can begin to find hope in the beauty of nature and all its creations. We can work on believing in our goals and begin working towards realising our dreams. Together we will awaken the inner strength that you have been dampening for so long. You will find your true self and learn how to look ahead once more. It will take a while, but I am sure you will get there, dear stranger.

From your friend, the hopeless romantic.

DAY 11

if you're given darkness,
you'll also be gifted with stars.

ABOUT PATIENCE

Dear Stranger,

I hear the impatient tapping of your foot or hand against any surface you can find. I sense the frustrated torment of your thoughts as you try your best to calm yourself. I know that life has been tough and that every hurdle in your path has seemed almost impossible to overcome. But keep on being patient; your time to shine is on its way.

It will require perseverance and, on some days, sheer stubbornness and determination. But you will get there. Wherever that is, for you. One day, you will stop and realise that after trying your very best to be patient for so long, you are exactly where you want to be. If it's a job, your perseverance through the training and interviews and your commitment to furthering your knowledge and skills will aid you in achieving that dream. If it's a family, your patience while building and nurturing it will bring you a peaceful and love-filled future. If it's overcoming a setback that has been troubling you for a while, like an illness or a bad time, your patience and perseverance in the process of healing will be your life raft through the murky waters of bad health or negative experiences.

I know you've got it in you. I have seen you battling your impatience and getting frustrated when life throws you one curveball after another. I know what that fight feels like. I know you feel like giving up on some days, and that sometimes it feels like too much to keep fighting. But I know you can. Keep going. Persevere through the murky waters of life. Swim against the rapid tide. Do your best to dive under the biggest waves. Use all the energy in your arms to swim fast and hard against the current. I promise, your determination to get to the other side will be worth it. When you feel weary, it's okay to tread water for a while. But make sure you keep fighting when you most need to. Navigate those stormy seas and soon enough you will find your own version of a calm, sunny day. You might be exhausted when you get there, but I am certain you will feel that all the hard work and determination was worth it in the end. Like the sensation of coming to the surface after swimming underwater for a long time, when you can finally take a deep breath of air into your lungs again. That is worth all your patience, I promise you.

No matter how often life gets the upper hand, the sheer will to work towards your goals and overcome your hurdles will be your biggest strength. You have more will power than you realise. And if you feel like you don't, reach out to someone close to you. We have all experienced setbacks, and we have all had to put in the work to get what we wanted in life. It takes work to get better even from an illness, whether it be physical or mental. Whatever it is, if you need support, I am here for you. I am here to listen when you need your worries to be heard. I am here when you need a shoulder to cry on. I am here when you need a helping hand over that last hurdle. I am here when you feel weak, as if all your resources are drained. I will provide you with the support and encouragement you need to regain momentum. I can help you see your own potential and your true worth. You have me by your side to lighten your load on life's long path. Reach out and ask for support if you need it. We are all fighting the battle of life; we cannot do it alone and find happiness at the same time.

The love of others will help you to find love for yourself. Give and receive love as much as you can, and you will find the inner strength to master patience and develop your perseverance. You are not alone in this struggle; we are all struggling to manage amidst life's worst situations. Don't rush yourself and don't rush through life. While you learn how to be patient, you may also learn how to enjoy each moment for what it is. We must embrace our environment and make the most of what we have, while balancing a need to not remain stagnant in life. I know you have the capacity to love everything around you. I know you also have the capacity to achieve your dreams if you put your mind to it.

The home you have always dreamed of is within your grasp. The family you have always hoped for is right around the corner. The career you have always imagined is just ahead. The lifestyle and friends you have always longed for will come to you. You will have it all if you are patient and work hard to surmount the barriers separating you from your goals. Nothing comes easy in life; but then, nothing worthwhile ever does. Keep fighting, and you will find that your will power is the rocket fuel that will take you anywhere you want to go.

Do one small thing every day towards moving forward, to embrace your life and discover your inner strength. One small step every day will aid you in finding your potential and motivate you to reach out further towards your dreams. Everything is within reach, if you just try for it.

In the meantime, patience, my friend. Your time will come and life will seem brighter.

Sending you all my patience.

DAY 12

maybe we will never meet
but we can still walk together
like parallel lines
to infinity and beyond.

ABOUT FORGIVENESS

Dear Stranger,

You have a deep wound that feels as if it will never heal. It started as a pain, a sense of betrayal that hurt so much that you thought your chest would burst. When the initial pain left you, you felt resentment and anger. An anger that was perpetually fuelled by memories of what had been done to you. What had started as a small flame that burned you and taught you to be cautious now began to burn out of control, a raging inferno that threatened to raze you to the ground. The wound, once just a small burn, festers and oozes. It makes you ill. You know you should treat it. Instead, you pick at it, adding more fuel to the fire.

I see you struggling to stay detached—trying desperately not to feel the flames, trying to ignore the fire you have ignited by holding a grudge. But you can sense the heat against your skin; it fills your belly and reddens your cheeks. Instinctively, you know that it is dangerous; that it is wrong. But you are mesmerised by it. Consumed with the anger inside of you, you are drawn to the flames like a moth to the light. You know it will burn you, and that if you allow it to, it will destroy you, snuffing out all that is needed to form a meaningful bond with others. Trust, love and peace will be replaced by nothing but destructive bitterness. I know you have tried to forget what they did, that you have even justified it. But the fact remains: what they did caused pain. Real pain that is lasting. Pain that has changed you irrevocably. And so, you create more fuel with your resentment and stand aside, watching the flames burn brighter, hotter, destroying everything in their path.

I want you to know that I too have been wronged. Wronged in ways that fundamentally changed who I am. Violated, mentally and physically, destroyed by someone I trusted. Like you, I built up my resentment until my grudges grew like invisible monsters in the night who told me I deserved what had happened. That, somehow, I was responsible for the behaviour of others. Systematically, you begin to shut those who genuinely care for you out of your life. The thought of allowing anyone else the opportunity to hurt you again is too much to bear. The monster grows; it feeds your thoughts of revenge and destruction.

The internal struggle between what you should do and what you want to do pushes you deep into the darkness. Your thoughts convince you that the only way to find peace is to hate the people who have hurt you. Hate the ones who caused you so much pain. You do your best to turn your back on the fire that is raging inside you. But hot coals spit forth, hurling themselves at you, burning, causing more pain, more suffering. I know you have tried your best to douse the flames. To move on from the collective destruction that has been caused. I know that you no longer want to feel this pain, that you want nothing more than to forget what has been done. To allow the natural rebirth that follows destruction to happen. But you feel powerless. The anger has become so deep, the resentment so all-consuming, that you are now only an observer, a bystander who keeps getting burned. Who continues to inadvertently fuel the flames and feed the monster. You feel powerless, caught up in your own destruction.

I am here to guide you through your anger. I want to help you let go of the resentment. To stop you adding fuel to the fire and to join you in putting it out so that it never reignites. I want to show you that the monster in your head that feeds your grudges can be moulded into a light-bringer, a source of positivity and hope.

Please allow me to guide you through the process of forgiveness.

Forgiveness is not forgetting what they have done to you. Forgiveness is acknowledgement. Acknowledgement that they hurt you, whether intentionally or by design, and that you had no control over their behaviour. I want to help you find acceptance that nothing you could have done would have prevented them from hurting you. Forgiveness is acknowledging that you may never be the same again, that owing to their actions you will not be whole again, but that life and beauty still grows from the destroyed and the incomplete. That a missing piece is an opportunity to create a new piece that can form something totally unique and different. I will be there to help you lift the burden of resentment that you have been carrying, and I will be there to pick you up when you collapse from the exhaustion this baggage has caused. I will be there to show you how to nourish your thoughts and fill them with acceptance. Today, I want you to understand that only you have control over how you feel and how you react, and then I want you to let go.

Because forgiveness does not mean forgetting, nor does it mean giving the ones who hurt you permission to re-enter your life. Forgiveness means that you simply refuse to allow what they did to you to control you any further.

I want to help you put in the hard work of planting new seeds and forming new relationships. Let me help you to learn to trust again. I promise you: you are not alone. And, once you forgive and let go, a new life can begin. One that is filled with love and light. No more flames, no more pain, only the beauty of the newly created.

Start living your light-filled life as early as today, dear stranger, and begin working towards a pain-free existence.

Sending you strength and courage.

DAY 13

i am not scared now
the pain has ended,
i am an ocean of memories
i have nothing to hide,
my words have defeated silence
i have nothing to lose,
i am chaos in its most beautiful form
i am the light of a darkened soul.

ABOUT HEALING

Dear Stranger,

I am proud of you. Proud that you've taken the steps to recover because I know how exhausting recovery can be. I know that the moments which brought you here were the hardest moments of your life, and that it took every ounce of strength to fight the urge to stay comfortable. Even if comfort meant misery. I know that at some point, not so long ago, healing seemed like a ridiculous notion. You didn't know exactly what would improve. You didn't even know if improvement was achievable.

You knew from reading the definition of 'recovery', that it refers to the process of restoring yourself to a normal state. But you did not know what a normal state was anymore. You had spent so much of your life in pain, wrestling the demons in your head, that 'normal' seemed far off. So far off, in fact, that it wasn't even a memory anymore. And that is part of the reason I am proud of you, because recovery in itself is reformative, and reformation takes work and sacrifice. I understand that the entire context of healing while you are grieving the loss of your normality is strange. It feels unnatural. And honestly, like you, I did not know how one could ever simply recover from a loss of that magnitude. After all, when you lose yourself, you would have to create someone new.

But you took the step; you chose to recover with the goal of healing. We know that even well-meaning people have questioned your process. That within a week people were already asking if you felt better. As if some magical elixir had been administered, some switch inside your brain found and turned back on. They do not understand that it took years of suffering to get to this point, and that it will take years of intense work to heal. That recovery takes a lifetime. I know that recovery means, literally, filling a void. Not a small, insignificant tear in the fabric of your life but a hole that has been torn in the universe of your mind. That no matter what happens next in your life, you will never be sure of success. I know that you will need to let go of the person you once were, and that in order for the healing to be complete, that person can never come back. I know you grieve for that person even though you know that they needed to be healed, and I understand why you do. I know that you are angry with the do-gooders and the well-meaning. That you want to unleash your building rage and tell them that at no point in time will you ever really 'recover'. That mental illness is no different from the loss of a limb. How callous would they be if they asked someone who had lost an arm if they had recovered it?

And you wonder, often, what 'healed' would mean in your case. I know that recovery is a tricky process. Its methods need to be malleable; it requires you to be mindful in order to apply the right kind of healing to the form your illness has taken right now. Mental illness, in any of its forms, is a multiple-headed beast. Just when you think you have a handle on how to deal with one of the heads, a new one decides to take its place. I understand that you are very new to your recovery, and that given what you have lost and what you are no longer allowed to restore, anger has become one of those heads. I want you to know that grief, pain and fear all bring anger with them, and that what you are feeling is normal. Allow yourself to feel your anger because it is a step in your recovery. Know that learning to placate each head of the beast brings you a step closer to healing. Recovery will mean dealing with the beast for a very long time, perhaps even for the rest of your life, but knowing how to handle the heads will mean that you have to expend very little energy on them in future.

I too have asked myself through recovery, 'What have I done?' Many times, I wondered what healing would look like if recovery never happened. When thoughts of derailment enter my head, I would ask myself: 'What would it take for me to live my life well, without recovery?' You see, I know now that healing is not possible without recovery. That opening your wounds to feel familiar pain will only prolong the inevitable. I hear you ask me what the inevitable is, and the answers are not pleasant. The inevitable is a life of pain, deep and visible scars, or the worst-case scenario: death. I want you to know that questioning your decision to start working on yourself is a normal part of the process, whatever normal means. You are worth that work. I want you to know that I am here for you, to help you through your recovery. Having tamed my own beast, I may be able to offer you some advice on how to placate yours. And because I know that no two mental illnesses are alike, I can offer suggestions on how to quiet your mind in order to begin healing. When those suggestions work, I will be there to celebrate your victory with you, and when they fail, I will help you strategize. I know that recovery is a lifelong process, and I will be with you every step of the way.

Together, we can take each day as another opportunity to progress on the path of healing. I will give you the strength you need to work through this process, and I know you will support me too, kind stranger.

Sending you strength and resilience.

DAY 14

you already know
i'm broken beyond repair
and still you hold me
as tight as you can
without letting me go
simply wanting and waiting
for me to undo the damage
i caused to myself.

damn it,
it's working.

ABOUT HEALTH

Dear Stranger,

Your health matters. You matter. Your body is an amazing machine that, given the chance, will provide you with a long life. You are wonderfully and uniquely created even if you do not believe it. Someone once told me that it should be liberating to know that among the 7.7 billion people in the world there is only one of me. That there are parts of me that have never been and other parts that will never be again. I know that right now you feel that many things in your life are completely out of control. That there are too few hours in your day to worry about your health. But looking after yourself is completely within your control. When you take care of you, you're able to take care of those around you. A healthy body and mind have the ability to perform in ways you would never have thought possible. I see you trying to keep up with life, to carve enough time out of your day to fit everything in. You have started neglecting yourself, and are beginning to become frustrated with how you look and how you feel. It is starting to seem like improving your health, both physical and mental, is an insurmountable hurdle.

I see you placing everyone's needs before your own, prioritising them above yourself. You believe that your needs should come last, but that couldn't be further from the truth. An empty plate is of no use to the starving, and because of that, you should be the number one priority in your own life. Nourish yourself. Maintain a nutritious, balanced diet. Choose to be healthy, but don't deny yourself all pleasures. Indulgences are a necessary evil from time to time. Those who tell you that everything is healthy in moderation are onto something, however, when it comes to food. If your body is well-nourished, you have the energy to get through the day. I understand that it is faster and easier to pick something up at a drive-through or pop a frozen meal in the microwave, but ultimately your body will begin to fail. Because your energy reserves are filled with fuel that do not sustain you in the long run. Eventually, you will become lethargic and tired, making it all the more difficult to get through the day.

Nourish your mind with positive thoughts and build a constructive internal dialogue. Don't allow yourself to think negatively. Remember, you are an amazing being. Fill your brain with enlightenment. Read. Never stop learning and never stop asking questions. There are no silly questions. There is only the quest for knowledge. At the end of the day, take the time to clear your mind of its clutter, and allow yourself to recuperate without guilt. Practise calming techniques and meditate. When needed, seek out professional help. Never be ashamed to put your mental health high on your list of priorities. Remember that a clear mind is a calm mind. If your thinking lacks clarity and you are unable to process your emotions, you will soon begin to feel overwhelmed and no longer be able to handle life's daily grind. Caring for your mental and intellectual well-being ensures that you are able to cope better with the stresses of everyday life.

I understand that physical activity means carving out more of your precious time, but if you find a form of exercise that you enjoy, it will become something you look forward to. Keeping your body fit will help keep your mind fit. It also allows you to bond and create meaningful relationships with people who love to do what you love to do. You will become physically stronger, your confidence will grow and your self-image will improve. I know that it is difficult to initiate a daily regime of physical activity, and that you fear rejection or humiliation, but the truth is, we all started somewhere. Eventually, you could even motivate others who are in the same place you were in once. When you begin to neglect your body's well-being, you allow illness to take over. Believe me when I say, I know what it means to feel sick all the time.

How you feel matters. Stop searching for happiness in all the wrong places. If it doesn't make you feel good, if people around you are affecting your energy negatively, cut them out. Your happiness will be affected if you continually allow negativity in your life. You will begin to feel drained. If you are constantly expending your emotional energy on those who do not deserve it, you will neglect those who do. Don't forget, that includes you. I understand that it isn't easy at times, but remember, loving yourself is as important as loving the people you've chosen to have in your life. Self-love is the basis of happiness.

I know what it is like to feel disconnected from yourself, to be unsure of what sets your soul on fire. Take the time to reconnect with yourself. Meditation will help you to calm your mind, bond with your inner self, and will create self-awareness. When you allow yourself to be disconnected spiritually, you begin to lose the sense of who you are, and what once stirred joy will leave you with a sense of emptiness. Knowing who you are and being connected spiritually will give you purpose in life once more and connect your healthy body and mind to a healthy soul.

I believe in you, and in your capacity to change your life for the better. Take a small step today towards turning your life around because you deserve to be the healthiest version of you. One step a day in the right direction will make all the difference.

Live life to its fullest. Happiness is a choice. In this moment, right now, you can choose to feel joy. Remember, you only die once. You live, every single day. So, start with today.

From your body and mind.

DAY 15

you think
no one can fix you
but you don't know
some prayers are powerful
and some souls know magic.

ABOUT POSITIVITY

Dear Stranger,

I know you are tired. Tired from swimming through the depths of depression. The feeling of melancholy is so overwhelming that it consumes you. The people who love you have been trying to pull you out but the negativity drags you back down continuously. It seems to be everywhere you look. On television, in the media, and deep down inside. Your fragmented mind seems to play every negative event back to you on a loop. It tears at your soul and destroys your character with every word of self-hatred it spews. I am no stranger to this feeling. The feeling of an ocean of negativity washing over you, pushing you under, further and further, until eventually it feels as if you will never break the surface and breathe in the air you need to survive. I know that this negativity is an unwelcome darkness—that it follows you around, hiding in the recesses of everyday life, waiting to pull you back into its churning whirlpool. You feel like a victim; you do not understand why you are forced to feel this, to carry this burden. Hopelessness surrounds you because you notice only that which is negative around you. A sense of impending doom fills your mind, and you know that everything you see will affect how you speak to yourself. You know your thoughts will start their downward spiral into self-loathing and hatred.

I see you get out of bed today with renewed determination. I know that, deep down, you realise that you have a choice. That the waves of crushing negativity are self-made, and if you could just stop thrashing about in the water, it would be calm enough to swim to shore. That you do not have to be at the mercy of your mental states because you have the ability to control your mental health. I am with you on this path—I know that it can be a bumpy ride. Finding positivity often entails taking twists and turns through unfamiliar and dangerous territory. I too crashed a couple of times before finding the right path—the turning point in your life where hardship no longer seems to be the only choice. I am with you as you change your mindset, and I applaud you for acknowledging that it is your attitude which affects the way you see the world.

I see you writing in your journal. Making the conscious effort to record everything good and positive that has happened in your day. Acknowledging that others who suffer the way you do have been able to make it through to the other side. You know that the change will not happen overnight, and that it is easy to fall back into the trap of negativity. You understand that the past can never be undone and you accept that changing your mindset will take hard work. But you are doing well because you have realised that you have control over your thoughts. Control over how you react to all that is negative around you.

Believe me when I say that emerging from the prison of my mind took time. My negative mind rejected the very concept of positivity at first. It took hours of positive affirmations, self-reflection and conscious avoidance of the negativity the mainstream media fed me, to prevent myself from wading back into that dark pool. I see the metamorphosis you are going through and I know that rebirth is never easy. Moving through this, making the journey from being a negative person to becoming a positive one, can be painful too. I see you working through the harm you have caused yourself and others, and I am here to assure you that it is human nature to lash out. Those who love you will continue to support you through this journey. Keep quoting your mantras when things get too hard. Willingly accept experiences that come your way, even if you do not like them. Life is about taking the rough with the smooth but always remember that you are in control of how you respond. There is much in the world to be grateful for; continue to look for it. When you see something that threatens to pull you downward, remind yourself of all the good things you have in your life.

Please do not give up your newfound path of positivity. The new people in your life, the ones who know nothing of your negativity or your past, can offer you a clean slate. They are just as important as the old people in your life, the ones who are celebrating your transformation into a positive person. New people do not have to be scary if you know that they can give you a fresh perspective on life. Never forget: everything that happens to you is in some way or another beneficial, if you allow it to be.

I am proud of you for not muffling your talkative mind. You have embraced the fact that it is what makes you unique and you have put in the hard work to reprogram it to positivity. Know that negative thoughts may re-enter your mind sporadically, but that is okay because your positive mind will dispel the negative, just like your negative mind used to repel the positive. Remember that your happiness depends solely on you. Celebrate the fact that you have come so far and rejoice in your change.

Know that you are stronger, wiser and better because you are on the path to positivity.

Take a moment each day to celebrate your progress (no matter how small), because what matters is that you are moving forward. Keep going. I know you can.

Sending you positive vibes.

DAY 16

i wanted my life
to have a tragic ending
so i could write about it
dwell and drink in pain
tell people about it
and make them cry
sell my sorrows
and become famous,
i so wanted it!

but then one day
i met you
and you gave me
a happy ending.

damn you, my love!

ABOUT SECOND CHANCES

Dear Stranger,

Second chances are hard, not just for you, but for the people around you. I realise that you have already been through many trials and tribulations, and that you have done all that you can to heal yourself. You are ready to give yourself a second chance at life. I understand that you are apprehensive because second chances mean that you are allowing yourself to be hurt again. That your newly healed heart, still cracked and bruised, will have to subject itself to the possibility of pain again. I know that a second chance means returning to life and putting yourself back in the same situations that hurt you to begin with. But this time, you will be different. Better equipped to deal with those situations. You will have learned to set boundaries. You will know that sometimes people don't hurt you with intent, and at other times they act out of malice. This time you will understand that you are in control of your own emotions, but not those of others, and because of that you will be strong enough to enforce the boundaries you have set and walk away.

I need you to know this: because you are now aware of how you used to feel, you will not make the same mistakes twice. You now know not to disrespect yourself like that ever again. You know that you have raised your standards by learning how to cope. That you have educated yourself, and cultivated a genuine respect for the person you are and for the person you would ultimately like to be. I understand that you were brave enough to begin to love yourself again, despite your flaws, and that you have also come to accept that those flaws are what make you completely unique. I see that you have put effort into forgiving yourself, even if you weren't quite ready to do it just yet. I have seen you come through your suffering, letting go of the weight that pulled you down for so long, rebuilding yourself. That took strength and courage, and I am proud of you. I want you to know that you deserve this second chance. I see you, still suffering from time to time, and I know you sometimes feel that life isn't fair. That your second chance, earned through so much effort, should be filled only with positivity and light. I want you to know that I am here to help you through those moments and to guide you through your second chance.

Remember: while giving yourself a second chance, you need to ask others to do the same. I know it is embarrassing, but I will be there to offer you support. I will be with you when you cut out all that is negative and toxic in your life. I will be your shoulder to cry on when people you expected would support your second chance are apprehensive or unwilling. I do not want you to be discouraged by their behaviour; do not get sucked back into the negative void that you have just come out of. I do not want you questioning the reasons behind your recovery; I want you to continue to see yourself differently. As the strong, confident person who deserves this second chance.

I want to be there, to set a good example for you. To remind you, and in doing so remind myself, that recovery is brave and takes more strength than most are capable of. You do not deserve to go back to what you were living through. Where you are right now, even if it is still tough and raw, is exactly where you should be. I understand that you are terrified of falling down the rabbit hole again. Of not being able to come out this time. But, this time, I am here, guide rope in hand, and

I will not let you fall again. All you need to do is call out to me, and I will help you.

I want you to know that you deserve this better kind of love. This realistic love that has enabled you to love yourself unconditionally. That you deserve the words of kindness you are speaking to yourself, and that those who love you, those who really care, will speak those words of kindness too. I know that the terror of your heart being violently crushed is still fresh in your mind. That the war which had raged in your mind for so many years still produces casualties. I too tried desperately to crawl back into the familiar, away from my second chance. But I also knew that the familiar would mean pain. That the work I had put in would mean nothing, and that the confidence I had built as a fortified wall against the negativity of the world would come crashing down. So, I reached out in the same way that I want you to. When it feels like the void is sucking you in, when you feel that the war may begin again in your mind, when you speak words of hatred about yourself instead of words of love, please reach out and trust me. When your boundaries begin to blur, when your mind begins to ache, and you doubt whether you deserve a second chance, trust me. Take the leap. Embrace your second chance.

Trust me.

If you start embracing your own second chance, maybe at some point in the future you will be able to love yourself again.

Sending you never-ending love, dear stranger.

DAY 17

'What if I never find love?'
'Don't worry. Then, love will find you.'

'How?'
'In its own mysterious and magical ways.'

'Why?'
'Because souls like you deserve to be loved.'

ABOUT LOVE

Dear Stranger,

Love is a formidable force that consumes us. Love was never meant to hurt, nor was it meant to cause harm. It was meant to nurture and help its recipient grow. It has the power to make us believe that we are the most important person in the lives of those who love us.

Romantic love, like life, evolves. It grows from passion and lust in its early phases, to support and the creation of new life, and eventually, in the twilight of one's life, into companionship and kindness. Romantic love is meant to intertwine your spirit with that of another. Experiencing an extremely strong connection with your partner can make you believe that life without them would be dramatically different. Have you felt the raw passion and connection that comes with falling in love with someone? Whether it is the first time you have experienced it, or it has happened more than once in your life, finding someone to love feels all-consuming and magical. I know how that feels, dear stranger.

Yet, when stressed or wounded, human beings can inevitably lash out at the ones they love the most, because we know that those who love us back will forgive us. And, although they are hurt, their love will enable them to look past what we have said and done. You've probably been at the receiving end of that, just like I have. But this is not how it works in romantic love. When romantic love turns into a force of destruction and pain, when they lift their hand to strike you, when they call you names and throw around wild accusations, it is not love anymore. I know that your love for them is so great that you forgive. I know that the pain in your chest and the chaos in your mind far outweighs the physical pain they have caused. I know that the thought of severing ties terrifies you, but dear stranger, romantic love is not meant to hurt all the time. Be brave, take the first step, and take your life back. It will be hard in the beginning, but leaving will mean that you at least have the opportunity to find true romantic love. One that nurtures and feeds you positivity, and allows you to grow once more. One that you can reciprocate in kind and share common ground with.

Family love is a love that we are told is unconditional. A love that nurtures us from conception, even as we grow in utero, and into adulthood when we start our own family. Family love is pure and good. It does not judge. Romantic love may be the source of our creation, but family love is supposed to be constant in all our transitions through life. Not all of us have had the privilege of receiving the ideal kind of love from our families. At its best, it is a guiding, nurturing and formative love. It gives you the sustenance to begin your life and it gives you the strength to continue through it. Like a potter moulding his clay, family love should create something beautiful, unique and unforgettable.

I know that some do not have the good fortune of experiencing family love. That your mother, who incubated you, did not want you. I know that some of you have lived, are living, in a place you cannot escape. I have been there too. Where your family, instead of nourishing you, threatens to tear you down. I see you, hands over ears, crying, pleading for a different life. Hold on. You can survive this. The beauty of family love is that you can create your own, and in nurturing your own family you will know what pure love is. Your new family, your chosen family, will heal you. Dear stranger, family love does not allow family members to touch you inappropriately. It does not give permission for you to be beaten or emotionally torn apart. Family love in its true form begs to make you whole, so please reach out and allow them to help you.

The love you receive from the people you have chosen to bring into your life as friends is a Platonic love. That of your confidants, your chosen people, your tribe. A love that requires no deceit, no concealment, no masks. This means you can fight, not speak to each other for months, and yet pick up exactly where you left off when you make up. These are the people you call in your darkest moments and celebrate with when you are happiest. Platonic love respects boundaries. It understands that friendship is outside the constructs of the family dynamic as well as the romantic relationship; it is a relationship that allows you to set the rules. I have built my own family love from Platonic relationships.

Find the sibling you always dreamed of having in your best friend, help them to raise their children, and create your own family. There are no expectations, and because of that, there is a greater level of forgiveness and a greater level of acceptance for human flaws. Platonic love is a selfless love; it understands that loving is mutual and should benefit both parties. Platonic love does not push past boundaries that have been mutually decided on. It does not expect you to cross the line into romantic love, nor does it pressure you into sexual gratification. Platonic love is supportive, not derogatory. It understands that constructive criticism is needed but constant criticism is not. It does not tear down personalities or wound the self-esteem. Those who seek to hurt you do not love you.

The most important love is self-love. Dear stranger, self-love is the only love that will ultimately carry you through your journey in life. If you cannot love yourself, you will never fully accept the love of others. Despite what you have been told, self-love is not selfish love. You are not selfish for choosing to care for yourself. It took me a long time to realise this, especially because we don't expect to suddenly feel love for ourselves after so many years of self-hate. Self-compassion is necessary to be able to survive the cruel world we live in. Learning to love yourself means learning to love all aspects of who you are and embracing that which has happened to you. It is understanding and accepting that you are human, and therefore, in some way or another, fundamentally flawed. But this does not mean that you are permanently damaged. When you learn to love yourself, you accept that your flaws make you beautiful and unique. Love yourself, dear stranger, love everything about who you are. Stop telling yourself negative things, and stop worrying about what you cannot control. Know that you are worthy of all kinds of love, in their purest, most wonderful forms.

Remember, love is a formidable force. Use it to create joy and happiness, and the acceptance of those who love you. Love yourself. Please. Love yourself. With every breath, with every heartbeat, with every fibre of your being. Love yourself.

Begin working on loving yourself today, and every day after will begin to feel a little easier.

From a loving companion.

DAY 18

i am your home,
you'll always
come back to me,
always.

ABOUT FAMILY

Dear Stranger,

I know that you are not able to accurately express how your family—including your friends, your chosen family—have helped you during your journey. I know that at one point you realised you had a good life, and that they had provided everything you needed and so much more. You were never able to describe accurately the fact that these things—the house you lived in, their love, your schooling, college education, and your job— were for you a safety net that both comforted you and pulled you deeper into your depression. I know that for the longest time they described you as a happy person and you did not have the courage or the strength to tell them that you barely had enough in you to keep your head above water. If it wasn't for them, you would probably have succumbed to the currents pulling you down. That the currents creep in and suck you out to sea, taking hold of you despite your possessions, your status, or the people who love you. You were never able to tell those around you that being caught in a current was a comfortable place to be, that despair and hopelessness were the only forms of emotion that you remembered feeling. That you loved them, but no longer in a way that burned with intense joy. Rather, love had turned into a feeling of obligation through guilt.

I can't accurately speak of your specific demons, but I can tell you about mine. I know that the rational side of me understood that I had a problem, and that my life was good otherwise, but the irrational part, the part occupied by my demons, told me that my problem was not curable and that I didn't deserve the love and adoration I received from those around me. That I couldn't possibly enjoy something I did not deserve. The default setting in my mind was communicating that life would be better for those around me if I was no longer here. I remembered growing up hearing people say that suicide was selfish, but I thought it was brave and I was nowhere near courageous enough to release my family from the misery I caused them daily. The only thing that pulled me through those moments was knowing that the pain I would cause by taking my own life would far outweigh the pain I was causing by continuing to exist.

What pulled me through to the other side was remembering what I had lived through as a child. My father not being around, my mother desperately trying to make decisions that included me. How she tried to integrate me into a new family with a man who clearly favoured his own children above me. I wanted to be given the opportunity to do better, to rise above what had been done to me. I wanted the chance to forgive my mother, and to acknowledge her love and sacrifices for me. I wanted to be able to give my stepfather a chance to love me instead of rejecting him, and I wanted to be able to forgive my father for abandoning me when I needed him most. This was the extra motivation I needed to cross the final hurdle on my path of healing.

I understand that your family dynamic may not be the same as mine. That your childhood may have been one that was filled with love, like the dream I had of a whole and complete family. I don't tell you my story to fill you with guilt; I understand that your story is different. Love and stability from your parents and family are not always enough to placate the demons inside. But I have to assume that you are still here, still reading this, because they are an integral part of your journey to recovery. Whether active in the foreground, or standing quietly in the background, your parents and family will play a role in your recovery because they were a part of your upbringing. Although they may not have contributed to feeding your demons, they are still there to help you battle them. Your battle may mean that you have to forgive, to let go of the anger and resentment you have held on to for so long. You may have to work on overcoming the abandonment you feel. Perhaps you will need to ask for their forgiveness or allow them to love you in the way that you deserve. There may even come a time when you will have to decide whether you want your parents and your family in your life, or if their presence will only serve to feed your demons. I want you to know that there is no shame or guilt in letting go of anyone, regardless of genetics, if it means that you are able to heal and live a happy life.

Know that family is not always formed by ties of blood, that leaving behind the people who raised you, or abandoned you, does not mean that you will be alone. You have the ability to create a chosen family of people who will love you unconditionally. Your friends, although not related to you by blood, are also your family; they will be there to help you through this. Regardless of where you are now, you are capable of doing better and being better than your circumstances. Know that, in a healthy family unit, you are allowed to love and be loved, and that you have the ability to carry forward that love as you grow and create your own family. If you weren't that lucky, I want you to know that someday, somebody will love you unconditionally. That they will need you as much as the air they breathe, and that you will have the chance to undo the wrongs done to you. If you allow yourself to heal, you can do better and be better than you thought you deserved.

With your loved one by your side, taking one step forward each day will feel much easier. You will be supported and cheered on to the best of their ability. Embrace the love. Feel it. You deserve it.

From a loved one.

DAY 19

if all you want is darkness
i can rip out all the stars in the sky
but i'm sorry
my heart cannot stop glowing for you.
you can have a starless sky
and a moonless night
but i'm sorry
my soul will always send you light.

ABOUT FRIENDSHIP

Dear Stranger,

You were told when you left home to go to school that you would make friends. When you came home, often feeling sad or lonely, you were told to make friends. But I know that finding friends who last, and finding people who help hold you up, can be difficult. Not everyone is lucky enough to find true friendships early in life, but this does not mean that you won't find them. Once we reach adulthood, it can be difficult to find ways to build connections; we no longer have spaces like school where we encounter like-minded people. Some of us, including me, find it hard to go out and forge new connections with other people.

But don't give up hope; try and put yourself out there. If you feel lonely, try joining a gym or taking a class you are interested in. Try open mic nights, if you enjoy music. Go to yoga classes. Join a football team. Attend poetry readings. Volunteer to work for a charity. Participate in community events. Try getting an allotment and connect with other gardening enthusiasts. There are routes out there for all of us. We just have to try.

True friends are hard to come by, but it isn't impossible to find them. Don't settle for toxic relationships. Your friends should keep you smart—encouraging you to learn more, do more, be more. To keep up with them, to have a meaningful relationship where you are both on the same level, you must actively seek out knowledge and experiences. Together, you should help each other expand your intellect and progress together. Search for people who lift you up when you need it, rather than those who shut you down. Take the time to thank them for all that they have done for you.

Friends can help you survive devastating health issues and pull you through your darkest days. When you are supported, when you know without a shadow of a doubt that there are people who are prepared to carry you through your sickness, you have a greater chance at survival. Your career will flourish because of your friends. They will encourage you by pushing you to take chances you wouldn't normally take. Because of your friends, a promotion you wouldn't have bothered to apply for, could now be yours. They will support you while you quit your bad habits and cheer you on from the side-lines when you run your first mile. Your true friends only want what is best for you. Listen to them; accept that they are not criticising you. Listen with an open mind, to avoid conflict with the people who care about you most. Accept that they are guiding you towards becoming the best version of you. Let them lead you, but do not always be led. Accept the guidance and the support as another opportunity to feel loved and valued. Your friends are your family, so maybe take a moment today to tell them you love them.

Friends will teach you more about yourself than you know. My closest friends have taken the time to get to know me on a deep level, and I will forever be grateful for the times they have been able to save me from myself. I'm sure you feel the same way too, dear stranger. They have chosen to have you in their lives, and they have chosen to keep you in their lives. They know your strengths and your weaknesses, and they know how to help you overcome your problems. Meaningful friendships will help you re-evaluate your life. These friends are capable of providing you with insights about yourself without being critical and hurtful because they know exactly what triggers you. When the negative relationship you were in breaks down, they will hold your hand and pass you tubs of ice cream while you watch ridiculous rom-coms about failed love. And they will be there to tell you when it is time to stop mourning the loss of someone who did not deserve you in the first place. They will take you out and distract you while your heart heals, and they will be there to celebrate your new relationships. True friends are the ones you take shopping with you when you want an honest opinion. They are the ones who buy you the vanilla latte while you lament about being fat.

These are the people who grow through life with us, and no matter how much we change, or where we are, they remain imprinted in our hearts. My friends have managed to keep me sane; I'm sure yours have also had to bring you back from the brink of insanity. True friends are those we grow old with. The ones we tell stories about to our grandchildren, and those we share dreams with about our children falling in love and having their own families, making our bonds even stronger. My friends and I reminisce about the days when we were young and careless, about how we played games and danced in our bedrooms to distract ourselves from the dramas that came with teenage angst. They're the ones who walk with us down the aisle, the first to visit us when our kids are born, and the ones who help us stay when we want to leave. And as we grow into the twilight of our lives, they are the ones who support us through the loss of our loved ones. They will draw comfort from you in their losses too, as you do from them.

Give your friends love and treasure them. Find in each other the wisdom you have been seeking. Be a pillar of support in their life and they could be yours. Encourage openness and honesty. Avoid petty arguments. And if you do ever find yourselves in conflict, listen without judgement. Love them unconditionally and work through your disagreements with grace. Do not choose a path of drama and hurt. Find compassion and empathy for one another and work on fixing things. Just as they help you repair the damages in your life, help them deal with theirs, and work together to resolve issues.

Every day can be another opportunity for you to build strong friendships and create bonds with others that enrich your world and allow you to feel connected. Take each day as another chance to be a great friend to the people you love, and to accept kindness and friendship in return.

From your friend forever.

DAY 20

express before it's late,
love before it's gone,
feel before it ends,
hold before it leaves.

ABOUT SELF-AWARENESS

Dear Stranger,

I see you wake every morning in a fog of unhappiness. An utterly joyless existence that seems unending. You wake up stressed and in a negative frame of mind, in a state of fight or flight, and you don't know why. Your day has not even begun, yet you dread it. I know that, going through your morning routine, you feel detached—not emotionless, but desperately unhappy. I know you have always lacked confidence; I too have felt the damning effects on my self-esteem of having no faith in my own abilities or even the will to celebrate when I do achieve something. I know you don't like yourself, that you struggle even to maintain eye contact with your own reflection. Why wouldn't you? After all, the world has been cruel, and you think you are useless. I understand, dear stranger. It is okay to struggle with your self-esteem and doubt yourself on a regular basis. But maybe, once in a while, it would be worth trying to celebrate ourselves just as much as those we love?

You give all your energy to supporting your loved ones and leave very little left for yourself because you don't feel worthy of self-care. You don't focus on your own dreams because you don't feel they are worthy of consideration. You ignore your aches and pains because you don't feel that your health is important. But it is. If I was able to realise that I could begin looking forward in my own life, rather than looking forward for those around me, you can do the same. And no, caring for yourself doesn't make you selfish. No, it does not mean that you will neglect the people who are important to you. No, it does not mean that you are self-involved. It just means that you have decided you are important too. You can make the decision to move forward by living with intent, rather than out of habit.

You may lose some friends along the way, but I use the term 'friends' lightly here. Those individuals who make you feel guilty for dedicating time to your goals are not real friends. If they were, they should cheer you on from the side-lines just as you have done for them. They should give you the pick-me-up you need when you are low and frustrated. They should lift you up, not tear you down. As if you don't do enough of that yourself. You tear yourself down at any given opportunity, I know. Try to remember that others should be treating you the way you treat those you love, and if there isn't anyone doing that, then maybe you should try it yourself. Give yourself the unconditional warmth and kindness you share with the people you love. Think encouraging thoughts and come up with thoughtful ideas that put your own well-being at the forefront of your actions. You are a wonderful person; try to see yourself as you would see your best friend. I see you worrying about those you love, caring for them, going out of your way for them; try and do this for yourself. You deserve to feel the love you are so capable of giving.

You have been told that happiness comes from within, but you have become convinced that happiness is an illusion. Because inside, you only feel sadness. A profound sense of unhappiness. In this state, it is almost impossible to believe that happiness exists at all. Like a child chasing the mythical creatures you were told stories about, you chase the unknown, never really sure if you will find it at all. You imagine a life where you are happy.

Finding happiness doesn't have to be a lightbulb moment where suddenly everything makes sense, and you love who you are and start to care about yourself. Self-care begins with small changes you make to your routine: maybe you run yourself a bubble bath once a week, or you go for a walk to help clear your head and reconnect with nature. Giving yourself the time to reflect on your day and how you are feeling in that moment will allow you to learn more about yourself. Just as you ask your friends how their day went, ask yourself about your day. Was it good? Was it bad? If it was a bad day, why? Are you not focusing on your goals enough? Perhaps you never set them in the first place. I've been there, don't worry. It took me a long time to learn to like who I am and build up my self-confidence. Nobody else can do this for you; only you can learn if you like who you are. Once you start listening to your internal dialogue, maybe you will figure out what makes you feel good. Maybe you won't, but you might at least have an idea that you want to explore. Delve into it, and build your confidence to work hard for the things you want, even if life doesn't always turn out how you want it to. Learn to love your experiences because they are yours alone.

I want you to listen to yourself, to the tiny voice in your head that has been trying to guide you out of your unhappiness. That voice is your intuition. It has been with you your entire life, guiding you. When a situation is wrong or uncomfortable, it gives you a gut feeling that tells you so. And when a situation is right, it fills you with hope and excitement. That voice is your subconscious mind, and it knows you better than anyone else. Listening to your inner voice is key in becoming self-aware and learning to love yourself. I want you to feel reconnected with who you are on a fundamental level. I want to explore what triggers you, what makes you feel less worthy of happiness than those around you, and then I want to help you control those feelings. I want to teach you that you have complete control over how you react to every situation in your life.

I learnt that sitting outside in nature as the birdsong quietens for the evening, the sun setting on the horizon, listening to the world, is a perfect opportunity to start listening to myself. I'm not saying this will work for you, dear stranger, but maybe you could give it a try? Or join the class you always wanted to attend. Go to the concert you always thought would be good. Visit that museum. Do all the things you have stopped yourself from doing for so long—from a lack of consideration for your wants and needs, or even a complete ignorance of your own desires. You deserve to treat yourself well and to love yourself.

As you figure out a good way to hear your own mind, embrace your own thoughts and act on filling your world with love and happiness. Try and look at yourself in the mirror at least once a day. I have been there; I know how hard it can be. But maybe if you look at yourself the way you look at those you love, you may be able to feel for yourself some of the love that you are so happy to give others. Look in the mirror as if you were looking at your best friend or your parents or your siblings or your partner. Look at yourself in the way you deserve to be looked at, and feel the warmth that radiates through you. I bet you are smiling at yourself now. Good, because it feels good to love yourself. Give yourself the time you deserve to figure out who you are, what you want, and who you want to become. Work on those goals; focus on your needs and desires. Stop listening to the voices telling you to be just like everybody else.

It doesn't have to be an endless and tiring mission; we can all start by making changes to our daily routines to help feel a little more cared for and a little more confident. Don't give up at the first hurdle; just keep listening to your own thoughts and feelings, and you will find your way. I'm sure of it. I want you to be happy and I want you to want to be happy too.

Sending you love and light for your reflection.

DAY 21

maybe it's not about
finding yourself,
maybe it's just about
loving yourself.

ABOUT PURPOSE

Dear Stranger,

You have been battling with yourself lately, not knowing what your purpose in life is. You feel as if you have been set adrift, floating at sea, waiting for the tides to take you along an invisible current that will wash you ashore. To a place you don't know, and don't fit into. You have contemplated the purpose of every other creature on the planet. Why it was designed in a particular way and how its purpose fills it with ease. How it never questions the conditions of its existence or asks what its purpose in life is. For instance, you see that a shark is created to keep the population of other predatory species down. Its job is to feed on other predators and to procreate. That is the sole purpose of its design, and it fulfils it effortlessly, without question.

I know that you think I am ridiculous for comparing you, a human being, to an animal, especially an animal that seems so basic and simple in its design. But think about this: what would happen if you removed its purpose? What if you caught the shark and put it in a tank, feeding it regularly so it wouldn't need to hunt? What would happen if you put it in an environment where it never has to use its instincts? I know that it is an animal, but what would its purpose in life be? Imagine that it never has to hunt, never has to breed or fight for its survival. At first, like you, the shark wouldn't care. Weeks would go by, with the shark quite content to be fed lifeless prey and not having to expend any energy in order to eat. But at some point, it would begin to show signs of anxiety and stress. It would swim around in circles, instinctively knowing that it was meant to be doing something but not knowing what. The need that it yearns to satiate is not hunger, you see; it is the hunt, the animal's driving purpose. And without this purpose, it will become depressed and eventually perish.

The shark in this metaphor is you, dear stranger. Your anxiousness and feeling of being lost come from your sense of purpose which is clawing its way out from deep inside you. The answer to your question about the purpose of your life is not an easy one, because there is no definitive answer. You see, like you, I questioned life. I questioned myself, and the meaning of this humdrum world we live in. Instead of answers, I found frustration.

I tormented myself, berating my stupidity for not paying more attention during philosophy class, for the lessons I had missed or was too preoccupied to care about. I researched and read. I sought counsel from men and women who were meant to be in the know. None of it satiated my hunger for the answers. I became self-destructive, depression crept in, and frustration gave way to a deep sense of loss. I mourned who I was supposed to be, even though I did not know who that was yet. Until, one day, I reached out to a friend. I expressed my sadness and frustration. My friend told me exactly what I am going to tell you. There is no one answer to the purpose of life. There are many answers. And you will have to find the one that resonates most strongly with you, because that is the purpose of your life.

Happiness, ever elusive in this day and age, could be your purpose in life. Search hard to find what makes you happy and pursue it. Once the source of your happiness is crystal-clear to you, you will find a sense of purpose in life. Remember that what makes you happy does not necessarily make me happy. Know also that others can be a huge part of your purpose. I discovered that helping others, even from a distance, fulfilled me. It closed a hole in my heart that I thought could never be healed. Leaving behind a legacy of happiness and positivity—

and I am not only talking about death, but even behind you in a day—will affirm that you have begun to know what your life's purpose is. This was particularly hard for me to realise, and I understand that it may be hard for you too. There is but one solution—love.

Love yourself fiercely, and love others in the same way. Acknowledge that you deserve to be loved. Love is a safety net; it is a soft place to fall when we are hurt or tired. Allowing yourself to be loved gives you refuge from life's storms; it is a means of being safe, away from judgement. When your emotional environment is safe, you have the space to explore your purpose. Many have told you, and I will tell you as well, that the purpose of life is to create. Not just procreation, but physical expressions and manifestations of how you feel. Art, music, dance, food: these are all creative forms that you use to show how you feel. Whether those feelings are positive or not, the purpose of creative expression is life's purpose—to heal suffering and release negativity. I want you to know that the purpose of life is positivity. To spread it, to speak it to others and yourself, to live it every day. It may seem underwhelming and barely worth the mention, but positivity is powerful. Positive thoughts, positive behaviour and positive actions lead to dramatic positive change. The purpose of life, dear stranger, is to create the meaning of your own life and then bring it to beautiful fruition.

All I ask of you, moving forward, is that you begin living life each day with the intention to find and create meaning, rather than existing through habit alone. By doing so, you will find your own meaning and create your own purpose for existence. And while you remain committed to this goal, you will never be alone.

Sending you wisdom and patience.

DAY 22

you think
your dreams are dying
but here's the truth
dreams never die.
they are simply leaving you
when they grow tired
they change homes.
they believe
they deserve better
because dreams love doers
more than thinkers.

ABOUT DREAMS

Dear Stranger,

Do you remember what it was like to dream? To believe with a wholehearted, burning passion that what you dreamed would come to pass. Dreams. They were a part of your life for as long as you can remember. When you were a child, you dreamed of floating amongst the stars, of walking on the moon, and of raindrops that danced as they fell. As you grew, so did your dreams. You played games that enacted what you hoped to become. Your dreams filled your head with ideas of what life would be like when you finally reached adulthood. As a teenager, dreams of princes and castles morphed into aspirations of doing well in your chosen profession. High-powered lawyers, CEOs and businessmen became your role models. You dreamed of travelling the world, of a successful career. Perhaps a family, in a house with idyllic picket fences.

Life eventually catches up, and at some point, somewhere, someone told you to be realistic. It probably wasn't done maliciously. It could have been a discussion about realistic expectations, qualifying grades or the scarcity of jobs that put your dreams on the back-burner. For instance, your hopes of becoming a prima ballerina were crushed by the lack of time to pursue your dreams and keep your grades up at the same time. As you emerged into adulthood, the choice of what to study no longer revolved around your dreams, but rather around your future pay cheque.

And so, the skills you were taught as a child, to help break your future down into steps and stages, begin to slowly erode your dreams. Pretty soon, they are forgotten. They become stories of what you thought you would be when you grew up, and seem to be a distant memory. Sometimes, you tell yourself that your dreams are still achievable, but just slightly out of reach right now. You will travel when your kids grow up, when they are in college, when they are chasing their own dreams. You convince yourself that there will be plenty of time once you retire. But then, after some time, you convince yourself that dreams are unachievable and hence useless, and eventually they are replaced with goals. You become more preoccupied with making your mortgage payments and making ends meet. We often re-label and compartmentalise what we once thought our ideal life would be, convincing ourselves that they were foolish aspirations to begin with. Enthusiasm and delight for the future is often replaced with apprehension and fear of failure. As our responsibilities grow, so does the reluctance to start a new life. To live our dreams.

Take the time to speak to any elderly person, and they will tell you that they wished they had the courage to follow their aspirations. To live their dreams. Not the dreams of becoming a princess, or of floating among the stars, but those that could have been achieved. There are no greater teachers than those who have already lived most of their lives. Find inspiration in those who are older and wiser, and take the necessary steps to put your dreams in place. Listen to them, draw from their knowledge, and reclaim your goals. Be your own greatest advocate. Dreams, no matter how you define them, can be achieved if you are prepared to put in the work that is needed. Speak positively to yourself; change your inner dialogue from conversations of fear and apprehension to those filled with hope and dreams. Begin to believe that you have a choice and reach out for that which is within your grasp.

Start small. Dedicate a part of each day to achieving your dream. Make your dream a reality, at least on paper. Create a vision board of what you hope to achieve when you succeed. Make sure it is visible every day and allow yourself to dwell on it. Then, act on it. Convince yourself that you can do whatever you set your mind to and don't allow yourself to be distracted by anything that doesn't bring you closer to your dream. Visualise what you want, in the same way that you did when you were a child. When you close your eyes at night, tell yourself that your goals are achievable. Don't allow negative thoughts to enter your mind.

In the same way, don't allow negative people to discourage you. You may lose some people you regarded as your friends on the way, and that is fine. Big thinkers and big dreamers attract like-minded people. They understand that holding down a steady job doesn't rule out being able to achieve your dreams. Remember that you have exactly the same amount of time in your day as everyone else. It is what you do with your days that will turn your dreams into reality. When things don't go your way, look for solutions rather than someone to blame. Set your plans in motion and greet every successful step with enthusiasm. Pat yourself on the back; never berate yourself. Take responsibility, not only for your successes but also for your failures. Understand that failure is an integral part of success. Behind every dream achieved, are obstacles that had to be dealt with. Treat setbacks as nothing more than hurdles. Remember that any obstacle can be overcome with a little strategizing and a change in direction. Don't get so caught up in the little things that you lose sight of the bigger picture. Be gentle with yourself, and allow yourself to learn and grow through your journey to achieving your dreams. Don't be scared of failure. Failure is an inevitable part of success.

Don't lose hope when things don't work out the way that you expected. You have grown and evolved; allow your dreams to do the same. Be mindful of the fact that all human beings have the ability to create. You may have temporarily lost the ability to mould your own destiny when you listened to the advice of those who told you to be realistic. It is still possible to reclaim your dreams. Create a journal, track your progress, and always be truthful with yourself. Accept and embrace your authenticity as a person, and then use it to your advantage. Don't let the fire in your heart burn out. Time waits for no man. There is no better time than now, this moment, to reignite your ability to dream. Book your ticket now. Travel the world. Experience everything you have ever dreamed of, and above all, never ever stop dreaming. Dream big, dream vividly. Dream, dream, dream.

Start dreaming today and your tomorrows will begin to look a little brighter.

Sending you creativity to awaken your dreams.

DAY 23

to love, survive and smile
are the hardest but
most beautiful things to do.

ABOUT HARD WORK

Dear Stranger,

I see you struggling through life, wondering how it got so hard. The principle of hard work is instilled in us from childhood. I remember being told that if I worked hard, I would be successful. That being the best at anything involved sacrifice. I was pushed to give my best, and it was expected of me to work hard. For me, hard work was associated with everything from careers and hobbies to everyday activities. I grew up believing that, with a great deal of effort and endurance, I would be able to excel at anything I set out to do. And when I turned the corner into adulthood, I believed those were admirable qualities. But like you, I quickly learned that hard work did not define success. That hard work did not only apply to the standard definition of success. When I discovered that, success began to mean so much more.

I understand the hard work it takes to fight your crushing depression. That squashing your suicidal thoughts to drag yourself to work every morning is hard work. That hard work is plastering a smile on your face and hoping that today will be a good day. That you have been fighting to stay alive for what seems like an eternity. I know that fighting your mind, the voice in your head that tells you that you are not good enough and that it wouldn't really matter if you ceased to exist, is exhausting. I understand that depression is not taken seriously, that employers often do not understand and that friends rarely know that you've lost all desire to live. Because I hid it too. I used to cry too, while putting that pill in my mouth to help me cope with my desperation. It made me feel weak and inadequate. Because I have come through to the other side, I want you to know that you do matter. That the world will be worse off without you. That seeking medical intervention is not weak. That you are brave and strong to do so. Above all, know that I acknowledge your hard work.

I see that it takes every ounce of your effort to get up in the morning. That it would be easy to just lose your way on your commute to work, but the thought of losing your job fills you with panic. That you feel like there are so many people around who seem to know more than you ever have, and that they make you feel redundant, useless and replaceable. I understand that it takes hard work to contemplate retirement, not knowing if all these years of work will support you for the remainder of your life. I see you balling your hands into fists while trying to deal with the debilitating fear that you will lose your job. The anxiety is so overpowering at times that you don't know if you will survive. You have quit so many times in your head that it takes all your energy just to show up every day and do what is expected of you.

I hear you when you tell me that hard work is taking on tasks that are not even assigned to you, not because it is expected, but because you need to feel relevant. Without these extra tasks, you fear the emptiness inside you will consume you whole. Or worse, it will allow the negative thoughts more space in your mind. I see that being the person everyone comes to with their extra work and emotional problems does not only fill the void but also drains you emotionally. I need you to know that I see your effort and your hard work. I know what it feels like to realise that, most of the time, no matter how hard you work, it will never be enough to put you in a position to succeed. I know this because I too felt like a failure, all the time. You are not alone when you fight with this constant sense of failure, of never being good enough. I understand that it no longer means anything when others say that you are successful. Because no matter how they view your achievements, you will never feel adequate, let alone successful.

I know you sometimes feel as if the colour of your skin, the sex you were assigned at birth or your sexual orientation will always count against you, and that it is hard work to pretend you are grateful for the opportunity to even be considered for roles of importance. That no matter how hard you work, how consistently you prove yourself, you will never be enough for them or for yourself. I hear you crying in isolation because people in positions of power think that it is their right to belittle you and that they can cause you pain with impunity. It is hard work to suppress the need to shout from the rooftops that you are being victimised, and it is even harder to resist the urge to retaliate by lowering yourself to their level. It is excruciatingly difficult to bear sole responsibility for the actions of other human beings, and to deal with their emotions without resenting them, while you are still trying to figure life out for yourself. I see how hard you strive to champion love in your community and patience and acceptance for others.. How much effort it takes to change the thinking of people who have known nothing but an inherent hatred!

Hard work is being expected to smile through all of this. This chaotic swirl of life, and the perfection expected of us. I know that, most of all, it is hard work to make people understand that the definition of hard work is not what it used to be. It is no longer about achievement or status. Hard work is about survival. About the will to live, the ability to provide for those you love, and being able to actually get through the day in one piece. Hard work is not about conforming to social norms. Staying alive, learning to trust and earning trust, and just being moderately functional, is hard work. I understand that, dear stranger, and I acknowledge your hard work.

Maybe you could start today by acknowledging your own hard work and celebrating yourself. It won't happen overnight, but in time that hard work may feel a little easier.

From a fellow hard-worker.

DAY 24

success should be the story
you would tell your kids
about the things
that made you happy.

ABOUT SUCCESS

Dear Stranger,

I know that you have put a great deal of effort into improving your life. You have followed all the advice and you have driven yourself to the point where you have attained your goals. Yet you still do not know whether you have achieved success. I see you struggling, not quite understanding what success really is. Not knowing if your hard work has resulted in an achievement that is solely yours, or if it is truly a success that you should share with others in your life.

I know you value the opinions of others, but I want you to recognise that your opinion matters too. That, in fact, it is your opinion of success and how you will achieve it that matters most. That people measure success differently and that the measurement of failure varies just as greatly. Hence, your opinion and your measure should be the only thing that counts as you move forward in life. I want you to know that how you define success will keep changing. That you have a defined starting point, but the finish line will never be clear. The fact that you are alive, breathing, coping and happy today means that today has been successful. When you get through a day without negativity and self-harm, and you can say that you are happy to close your eyes at the end of it, rest assured that it has been a good day. When you do not toss and turn anxiously in your bed all night, you have achieved success. These milestones *are* successes. And as the distances between them increase, as you set more ambitious goals, the success you attain will be greater. That success will be measured not only in your ability to remain happy, content and fulfilled, but also against what you wish to do in your life. I want to support you through this process. To enable you to change and grow and be happy permanently. I want to be there for you— at every single step on your path to successful recovery, to achieving your life goals, and becoming the new you.

I want you to know that success means you will need to continue to reach out, that you will need to continue to embrace the transformation that is happening within you. I want you to continue to focus on your health, to nourish your mind with positive thoughts and a positive internal dialogue. I do not want you to allow yourself to think negatively. Continue to fill your mind with enlightenment. Carry on reading and never stop learning. Expanding your knowledge was one of the reasons for your success to begin with, and continuing to do so increases your chances of success every single day. Continue to clear your mind at the end of each day so that you remain calm and can wake up tomorrow feeling fresh and invigorated. Do not allow shame or guilt to creep back into your life; self-love deserves admiration. Know that guilt and shame are the gateway to overwhelming emotions that will lead you down an incredibly dark path. Please, dear stranger, continue to nourish your mental health. Remember that success has an ever-moving finish line, and that it can be incredibly fulfilling to chase it.

I want to walk with you as you actively seek out your purpose in life, but I also want you to remember that everyone's purpose is different and that yours is what resonates most strongly with you at this stage of your life. Like the finish line of success, it will change as you grow. Never forget that the happiness you have worked so hard on is part of your purpose, and that it will often guide you on the path that brings you to your new purpose. Do not compare your purpose with those of others, and remember that your success can never be measured against theirs. You can use them as milestones, but never as measures. Remember those who stood with you when the going was tough, and understand that they will continue to be a critical factor in your current success as well as in your future achievements. They are the people you reach out to for advice and upliftment. They are the people who will give you support when you need it most. They, like me, will continue to rejoice in your successes. Appreciate them and allow them to guide you. Understand that they are not criticising you; they merely want to celebrate your next victory soon, being as invested in your success as you are.

I want you to know that, as I have suffered many setbacks on my way to success, I understand your apprehension about taking my advice. I had to learn what my stressors were outside of my protected healing environment, and face them head-on or avoid them where possible. I realised that what mattered ultimately was learning the ability to overcome those stressors. That enabled me to resolve my issues with some help from my support system, and prevented me from sliding all the way back into failure. That was, in itself, a success. I want you to be able to look back and to celebrate how far you have come because that will mean you have succeeded and will continue to succeed. Success, dear stranger, is whatever you define it to be. Celebrate it.

It won't happen overnight; you won't be able to feel successful as soon as you decide to. It will take work to reach that point, but when you do, dear stranger, you will begin taking every opportunity that comes your way to celebrate yourself.

From your devoted life coach.

DAY 25

you're not the sum
of all your failures
you're the multiplication
of every time you tried.

ABOUT FAILURE

Dear Stranger,

They told you that there could be no success without failure. That failure is, in fact, crucial to success. They said it is a necessary evil, the groundwork for eventually achieving your goals. That nothing worth anything comes easy. They said that your response to failure would be the true measure of your character. They have a lot to say, but they are not in your head. They do not live in the cesspool of negativity that is your mind. They don't fight the constant sense of inadequacy, or the fear that every endeavour will result in yet another failure. They do not struggle to accept their imperfections, waking up in the morning with the feeling that they are an impostor. That what they have to contribute to the world is a lie, or worse, that they are a complete fraud.

They said you should seek counsel in order to be guided out of your failure. What do they know; they have put you on a pedestal. They already see you as a success.

They believe you have picked yourself up and emerged unscathed on the other side. That failure, for you, is a minor setback. Part of the process. The truth is more painful. You spend your time over-analysing every flaw you believe you possess. You relive every defeat, dwell on your weaknesses and punish yourself. Your inner critic pulls you deeper and deeper into self-loathing until you go to bed, exhausted and defeated. You tell yourself that tomorrow will be a better day. That tomorrow you will succeed. But sleep does not offer you any respite either. You stare at the ceiling, and the scar in your mind plays back to you fractured pictures of everything that could have been, had you been adequate. The hole in your heart widens, and slowly, you begin to believe that you are utterly worthless. You try desperately to stop the loop that plays in your mind. Sleep does not come. You start the next day—exhausted, feeling worthless, and slipping into depression. You feel as if there is no place for you. Your family, your friends and your job will be better without you.

There have been days when you feel you may fit in. That this day may be a successful one. You begin the day comparing yourself to others. I know that you have tried your best to remain positive, to stop yourself from spiralling into self-loathing. But you know, deep down, that one mistake, one comparison, or the thought of a person who has done better than you, has the ability to catapult you into depression. A sense of inadequacy overtakes you, building in your mind. You know that your mind is playing games, tricking you into believing something that is not true. But I also know that your truth is different from what they see. I can see you struggling. Pushing down the anxiety that threatens to make you abandon your next project, sending you home from work to avoid having to take on any more responsibility. Your heart pounds in your chest. Fear takes control. I know that you do not want to be in the limelight. You do not want to be assigned anything outside of the scope of what you are confident you can do. And for you, confidence does not come easily. It is a daily struggle to convince yourself that you are worthy of where you are in your life. You don't believe that the people in your life have need of someone like you. You have convinced yourself that you are worthless. Nothing more than a sum of all your failures.

The truth is, you are worth it. You are more than your failures. You are certainly better than your opinion of yourself. Write a list of your accomplishments, no matter what their size. When you feel your mind begin to fixate on your failures, pull out your list. Read it;

reassure yourself. Prove to yourself that failure is only a part of who you are and what you have done. Instead of seeing your job as a daily torment, place yourself on the pedestal that others have put up for you. Realise that you are an integral part of your company's operation. Allow yourself to reminisce about your past achievements. They may be in the past, but that does not mean they are no longer relevant. Knowing you were able to accomplish them will help you realise that you are still a capable person. I know it is difficult to not compare yourself to others in a competitive world. I get it. But you have to stop.

You are completely unique, and because of that, you have something that other people cannot offer. Chances are, the very person you are comparing yourself to is struggling with a sense of failure because they are measuring themselves against you. I know that, once your feelings of inadequacy start playing on a loop, it is difficult to pull yourself out of it. For every negative thought you have about yourself, think of one positive. It's scary, I know. But the pattern works both ways. Trust me. The more you think of yourself with positivity, the easier it will be to see the positive parts of yourself. Reach out. Let the people who love you, help you. Talk to them and ask them if they feel the same way about you. Chances are, they will tell you that you are completely off-track. While reaching out, make sure to speak to those who know you well. Those who have been part of your history will be able to remind you about achievements you didn't even realise were significant. Never stop setting goals for yourself. Break them down into small, easily achievable steps. Praise yourself. Never stop praising yourself. You are unique; you are wonderfully created to be more than what you think you are. Failure becomes permanent only when you do nothing to bring yourself back in line with success. Believe in yourself in the same way that others believe in you.

It won't happen overnight. Begin believing in yourself today, and you will work towards finding your own version of success.

From a fellow failure.

DAY 26

the world would be
much better and more beautiful
and people would be
less lonely and sad,

if instead of asking,
'how are you?'

we said,
'i care for you.'

ABOUT KINDNESS

Dear Stranger,

Kindness, compassion and empathy—although seen as weaknesses by some and lately by you—are in fact the strongest human traits. These are the qualities that define your character in times of frustration, and lift you up in times of sadness. They constitute the inner strength that allows you to carry those who need it and are too weak to do it by themselves. They are also the foundation of self-love—a love that should be greater than any other, and one that you have long forgotten. I see you in despair, unable to understand what kindness is. You give an abundance of kindness to those around you, but you neglect to share that compassion with yourself.

You ask yourself continually what kindness is and I understand why you ask. In society today, it seems that kindness has been overtaken by cruelty, for people are so caught up in their own pain and their own lives that they no longer have the ability to be kind, to show any form of compassion or empathy.

Like you, I have felt a profound sadness which has made me lose hope in humanity. I too feel trapped in the web of war and other human atrocities, loathing myself because of it. I understand you believe that the same darkness which occupies the souls of others must be lying dormant inside of you, simply because you are human. The pain of others has begun to exhaust you and you have shut down. Blinkers on, you protect yourself from these visions of suffering, and kindness, empathy and compassion fall by the wayside as a consequence. You begin to harden yourself to others, and you are hard on yourself too.

You speak words of negativity in an attempt to convince yourself that you are no better than the unkindness you have read about or seen. I understand that you are not deliberately being cruel to others or yourself, but empathy means feeling—feeling your own pain, and that of others. Compassion involves working to help yourself and others. I know that you are exhausted, that you barely have the energy to make it through the day unscathed. That you feel guilty for taking the time to care for yourself above others. The guilt consumes you, and so the blinkers grow unchecked until they become an impermeable eye mask that does not allow in any visions of empathy, love or compassion. Your heart numbs and your mind turns its focus from kindness towards others to self-love. Apathy is a cruel monster. It will destroy everything in its path, including kindness for yourself.

I need you to know that empathy is a vital necessity. Not empathy for others just yet, but empathy for yourself. For the feelings you have, for the way you treat yourself. I know it is tough not to judge yourself too harshly, and to feel the full force of the emotions you have buried deep inside. But you deserve empathy for yourself, in order to be self-aware and kind. You may feel that you are expected to be perfect, but in reality no one expects perfection from you, other than yourself. Stop setting yourself up for failure; perfection is unattainable. Allow yourself to be flawed in every way that makes you *you*, and makes you feel human. Embrace those flaws wholeheartedly. Actively seek to be gentle with yourself, and take time to silence the critic inside your head who tells you that you are not good enough. Be compassionate and self-aware, and forgive yourself for shutting others out, for the behaviour within your control that caused failure, and for not allowing yourself to feel everything. Understand that you are not expected to help everyone all the time. But know that by opening your eyes to the suffering of others, you open your eyes to an opportunity to help. Know that I am here always, to help you find that compassion.

Kindness, in its purest form, does not need to stem from generosity or physical assistance. It comes from a place of self-awareness that allows you to be aware of others and of how you feel about yourself. It comes from learning to listen to your inner thoughts and allowing others to speak theirs. Kindness always begins with you. Start speaking kindly to yourself. In times of darkness, when you can find nothing positive to say about yourself, reach out to me. I will show you all the love and light that resides in you. Silence your inner critic by acknowledging that you have achieved so many incredible things in your short time on Earth, and if you cannot, I will help you see your worth.

Hold fast to your belief that humanity is good, in order to reconnect and affirm that you too are inherently good. If you feel that the cruelty and darkness is too much to bear, speak to me. Allow me to show you the good that is everywhere. Help others whenever you can; the smiles and gratitude of others will give you a sense of self-worth and prove to you that you have a purpose. Kindness towards others and kindness towards yourself can change lives. Don't forget that.

If you are not sure how you can make a difference, speak to me. I will guide you and be with you every step of the way. Remember, dear stranger, that you are worthy of love and kindness, from yourself and others. No one deserves cruelty, so the next time you begin to go down a spiral of negative self-loathing and self-cruelty, call me. I will show you all the reasons you deserve to be loved, because I acknowledge and love you. Above everything else, dear stranger, be kind.

Moving forward, be kind to yourself today, be kind to yourself tomorrow, and be kind to yourself every day.

Sending you kindness and compassion.

DAY 27

i wish i could be for you
what you have been for me
a ray of hope
a rain of happiness
a cup of coffee
and a book of love.

ABOUT GRATITUDE

Dear Stranger,

I am grateful for you and all that you offer to the world. I am grateful for your friendship and how you always lend me an ear when I need you. I am grateful for everything that you are. Your wisdom, your kindness, your compassion, your ability to understand how I am feeling, and your capacity to connect with others. You bring light into the darkest moments, and you provide a place of comfort when I need it most. When your loved ones need you, you are there to support, guide and love them. I hope you can learn to become grateful too. I am sure you feel grateful for your loved ones. I am conscious of your gratitude for the connections you have made in life, the love you have received, and the warmth you feel when you are understood and your feelings are considered. But I am not sure that you are grateful for yourself and the life you have. We can begin working on that together, I promise. You don't have to go it alone. I am by your side for this journey.

Continue being grateful, dear stranger. Be grateful for the earth and all it provides you. Be grateful for your mind and all that it challenges you with. Be grateful for the setbacks you face. Be grateful for your body that allows you to move and experience the sensations of life. Be grateful for your heart which keeps you alive. Learn to embrace your mind for everything it can offer, rather than focusing only on the negativity it sometimes brings to the party. You are in control of what you choose to love. Learning to embrace yourself one hundred percent for who you are will open your eyes and your world to possibilities you never knew were right in front of you. Learn to love yourself, and then begin learning to love life again. I know it is hard; I have wanted to give up too. But you can do it. I know you can.

Being grateful for ourselves can be the hardest thing we attempt to do in life, but also the most rewarding if accomplished. I am not saying that I have mastered this yet, but I am working on it. I hope you begin working on it too. You deserve to feel gratitude for yourself. You deserve to celebrate who you are. You deserve it all. And, today is not too early to start. Thank yourself for something you have done to enrich your life today. Maybe you made yourself breakfast; well then, celebrate your decision to fuel your body. Give thanks for the fuel and for taking the opportunity to nourish yourself.

Maybe you skipped breakfast but had a shower; that is okay too. Celebrate your decision to cleanse your body and look after yourself. You deserve to be taken care of, after all. Today could be the first day that you begin thanking yourself for life, the first day you begin working towards gratitude for your existence.

No matter how unlucky you feel right now, you are lucky to be alive. You are alive; your heart beats in your chest. It pumps blood through your body. Your brain sends signals to your muscles. Your organs communicate to function correctly. You are alive. Sometimes, we can get so bogged down by the small things that we can forget the miracle that is life. You once fought incredible odds merely to exist and be created as an organism, and now you are alive. You were created to feel joy, to feel pain, to feel love, and to feel empowered. You were created to feel. And right now, you may feel low. You may even feel hopeless. But you can feel other things too. You are capable of feeling happiness. You are capable of love. You are able to feel the positive things life has to offer. Be grateful for life and then use that gratitude to motivate you out of your darkness. Use it as a powerful tool to drag yourself towards the light again.

While you search for that light, no matter how dim the path may appear to you, be grateful for those who support you. Be grateful for your loved ones, whoever they may be: family, friends, other support networks, your community, your country, your world. Be grateful to those who celebrate your achievements and cheer you on from the side-lines. Be grateful to those who make you laugh and bring happiness to your world. You deserve to feel acknowledged and appreciated. Let them appreciate you. And appreciate them in return.

No matter how bleak things may seem right now, you can learn to find hope within the desolation. Choose to be thankful for your life. Thank yourself, thank your loved ones, thank the earth for all that it provides, and thank the universe for all the opportunities it puts in front of you and all the lessons it has provided in the past. Today is the day you choose to be thankful. Today is the day you embrace the life you have been given and begin moving forward with gratitude and acceptance for what will be.

I promise to be by your side as you move towards this goal. I will be there, every step of the way, to celebrate your progress as you do mine. I am thankful for you. I promise to help you to become thankful too.

A grateful friend.

DAY 28

the world has disappointed you
the universe will not.
trust me on that.

ABOUT THE UNIVERSE

Dear Stranger,

You have been questioning your purpose in life, but not just yours. You have been asking what the purpose of human life is. You have become consumed with thoughts of human cruelty and the human need to destroy. These days, it often seems as if people are caught up in a perpetual rat race. Like greyhounds on a racecourse, blinkers on, they chase a rabbit they will never ever catch, and you find yourself running the same race. Looking at the faces of strangers, it seems to you that they have lost their souls, and you ask yourself: do they even have souls? Do I have a soul?

Dear stranger, I too have questioned my humanity, and my ability to connect with life on a fundamental level. I too have built up walls in an attempt to guard myself against the cruelty that threatens to envelope all of mankind. I have fed myself unkind words and punished my mind with thoughts of destruction. I understand that you have lost touch with your spirit because I once thought that I had lost mine. I know that trying to find it leaves you exhausted, confused and emotionally hurt. So, you have convinced yourself that you have no purpose, and that the universe is nothing more than a tall tale told to children so that they do not fear death. But still … still you feel a nagging sense that there must be more. Still you have questions that you want answered.

I understand your questions about your place in the world and your connection to the universe itself. Does it all have a deeper meaning? Ask yourself the pertinent question of whether your life is really in your hands. You can control certain elements of it, but there will always be factors beyond your control. You must accept life's journey as the universe's way of teaching you the lessons you must learn to survive. The failure, the hurt, the heartbreak, the torment, the lack of self-esteem: they are all just life's lessons at work. Teaching you how to be strong and how to live on. They are milestones on your journey towards self-acceptance and happiness. You need to experience the bad to be able to appreciate the good. And the good is coming, I promise.

The most important thing I would like you to know is that the universe is multifunctional: the very fact that you are here, asking these questions, or that the sun rises and the tides flow, is because of the spirit of the universe. Everything that grows and expands is part of the journey of the universe; you too will experience this growth. It is coming to you. You are connected to the earth in ways you cannot comprehend. And you are connected to your loved ones and peers in ways that the universe has drawn out for you. Your path has already been designed, and you must walk along it to learn and grow and expand your mind.

I know you have many questions, questions that cannot possibly be answered in one day, but I applaud you for beginning your journey. Let the thoughts you feed yourself emerge from self-love, positivity and light. You need to have a firm grip on what is happening inside of your mind so as to nourish it properly. And once nourished, your mind will be capable of unfolding your own specific universe. I still hear you asking: but what *is* the purpose of life? The truth is, none of us will ever know, outside of the purpose of our own destinies. Follow yours; choose the path that will enrich your life, and learn to take control of it. What is important to know is that everyone needs to nourish their spirit in their own way. You do not have power over the behaviour of others. The only power you have is the ability to control your own behaviour and how you choose to react to the conduct of others. You have the power to control your thoughts. The power to nourish your mind, body and spirit with all that is good.

The universe connects us all, and we should embrace these connections to reach a place of understanding and knowing. You can learn to understand how we are connected, how we can help one another through life's lessons, and how we can affect each other's journeys. You do not have to walk this path alone. Find connections. Find people with whom you share common ground. Work together to build your paths, and begin working on your own idea of a journey. Begin working on your life.

I want you to know that I am here and that I do not want you to disconnect from your mind. I want you to know that feeling and working through your emotions is necessary to begin living positively. I want to be here to guide you through the process of self-enlightenment because it is vitally important for you to know who you are. I want you to ask questions; question everything. Accept the things you cannot control and work on the things you can. Life will throw you many curveballs, and thus, lessons will be learnt. Your very best life awaits you when you surrender yourself to the universe and begin following its guidance.

Start working towards your enlightenment today, and soon enough, your true potential will be awakened.

Love from your universe.

DAY 29

we must remember
that we are mere travellers of life
on our journey home,
that nothing will matter in the end
for everything is chaos
except love.

ABOUT LIFE AND DEATH

Dear Stranger,

What would you do if you knew you would die tomorrow? What difference would it make to you right now if you knew that your time here was limited? What changes would you make to your life in order to die satisfied, dear stranger? I know that you have been contemplating your mortality. That you have wondered if death would leave you satisfied. I know that asking you what you would do with a limited amount of time sends you into a panic that you would rather avoid. I too had an intense fear of dying. A fear that I wouldn't leave a great, or even adequate, legacy behind. I obsessed about what people would say. Would they say I had lived my life to its fullest? Or would they remember me for all that I had left undone.

I understand that, when it comes to death, you have almost certainly been indoctrinated into a culture of denial. You were raised to prefer not to contemplate death, the end of your worldly existence. I know that death was not discussed other than in mourning the loss of someone that you knew. Hence, all that you knew about death was that they were gone, that you could no longer see them, and that they would never come back. I understand that this instilled a fear of death in you. A shadowy figure waiting in the dark, holding a clock which never ceased ticking. The fear, when you were younger, was so great that you squashed all thoughts of what else death could be. Instead, you filled your time with life. With the expectations of others and the pursuit of dreams. I know there have been times when you have questioned your purpose, when you have questioned your soul, and wondered where you fit in, here on earth. The truth is, facing your fear not only serves to diminish that fear, it also allows you to contemplate life after your fear has been dealt with. Because of this, facing death means that you will be able to face life.

I know that you are struggling to contemplate a future in which you have not completed what you set out to achieve. That you are still striving to find your purpose. I want you to know that you are not alone. There are millions of people who battle with the same thought process every day. It is very difficult to envision your own future when you are not in it. When you imagine your future self, you feel detached, as if you are watching a two-dimensional character. The person that you will become is nothing more than a stranger to you. I want you to know that this is a completely normal response. But it will also prevent you from achieving your goals and reaching your full potential.

With a little effort, I was able to understand that without contemplating death I could never live a full life. I want you to know that the brain is re-trainable. I understand that the thought of change, whether it is positive or negative, is a terrifying thought. Because you have been programmed to remain comfortable, you feel anything that is new, or a challenge, may lead to failure. I was also afraid that contemplating death in order to re-evaluate and improve my life would send me spiralling into depression. That seeing how little I had accomplished in life would only serve to drive me back into my comfort zone.

I want you to imagine what your life would be like two years from now, if nothing changed. Do you feel that you would be happy with where you will be, not just from a physical point of view but from a financial, mental and spiritual perspective? I want you to be honest with yourself, and if the answer is no, I want you to tell me what it is that you would change. Then implement those changes tomorrow. I want to help you to see yourself at your best. I will hold your hand while you are critical about what you have achieved in life, but I will not allow you to be cruel. Write down the dreams you still want to achieve, create a vision board, and work with focus and determination to realise those goals. I want to help you visualise your future so that you are able to magnify your strengths right now. I want you to know that everyone has strengths, and no matter how many times you have tried to tell yourself otherwise, your strengths and your weaknesses are what make you unique. I want you to stop telling yourself that you are worthless, that life is hopeless, or that you have nothing meaningful to contribute to society.

When you look life in the face, you can embrace your pain and use it to live. Stare your pain down and take control of your instincts. You have control; don't let your feelings of helplessness trick you into believing the opposite.

I will take your hand and lead you on this journey of self-discovery. I will help you to achieve the greatness that you are destined to achieve. I want you to know that it is within your power to design your own life if you are prepared to accept that death is inevitable. That death can come at any time and that it is not what you were taught it was. I want you to know that envisioning the future empowers you to create something new. Something that is designed specifically for you. I am here with you while you contemplate your mortality and overcome your fear of death in order to become the best version of yourself. It will take much effort to master this, but I will guide you and hold your hand through it all.

Sending you the passion to live each day as an opportunity to learn more about life, and wishing you joy and happiness.

DAY 30

happiness is a daily choice
and not an impossible dream.

ABOUT HAPPINESS

Dear Stranger,

I know what it feels like to live in the darkness for too long. The clawing at walls and blind fumbling, trying to find a way out. The feeling that you will never see the end of this road. I know that you are striving to feel an emotion you once remembered, but now it seems so distant that it may have been a tale you told yourself. I know that you are terrified of the light. Knowing that it will burn your eyes and fearing that it will set your skin on fire because you have not felt it for so long. I want you to know that it will not be painful. Uncomfortable, yes, but not painful. That the discomfort is temporary, and that it is well worth it. That you owe it to yourself to be happy. Truly, deeply happy. The darkness is not safe; it never was. Being comfortable in pain is exhausting, and eventually it will drain you of your life. I want you to know that this darkness may have its purpose, but it should only be temporary.

I am proud of your determination. I see you getting out of bed quicker each day. I know that this is a victory. That lying there, dwelling on your sadness, is the easier option. I know that it takes strength and courage to dismiss the errant child tugging at your sleeve. To look it in the eyes and refuse to give it power until it changes its sadness and manipulation to something more positive. I see you making eye contact with yourself in the mirror, not detached but present. You are searching for the remnants of the person you used to be, and I see you decide that today you will be happy and present. Not the fake happiness you have been using as a horrible disguise for the longest time. You know the one: artificial smiles and courteous conversation. An endless play where you pretend to be who you were. Only you, and the people closest to you, know that the laughter never reached your eyes. That your smiling face would have preferred to bury itself in a pillow for comfort, burrowing into darkness or drowning in alcohol and tears. But now, I see you tell yourself that you want to be happy, and I believe you.

I see you making the effort every day, slowly banishing the waves of darkness. It eventually dissipates, turning into grey clouds that are no longer all-consuming, completely engulfing the light, but rather just dulling it slightly. Just ahead of you is a happiness that burns so bright that it will banish the clouds and bathe you in pure warmth. I see you tell the people who care about you that you are fine, good even, and that you mean it. Inside, you are beginning to feel good again. I am proud of you for deciding to spend time catching up with your family. I see you pulling these people back in with a genuine warmth and happiness in your heart instead of building a wall to shut them out. I know it isn't easy to trust that people will not hurt you again, and that they will accept you for the new person you have become. Today, you reached out to your friends; you did not wait for them to initiate the interaction. Instead, you asked if you could all go out, not because you needed to be distracted from your sadness, but because you are ready to make memories, to immerse yourself in laughter and happiness with your chosen family. You are no longer content to be nostalgic about a past when you were genuinely happy in their company; you want to be happy with them in the present.

I know you want to rush into this process; you want to be so happy that you wish to proclaim your happiness right away from the very rooftops where you screamed to release your pain. That you now expect your quiet, reflective places, where you used to go to feel grounded during your pain, to bring you a sense of peace and joy. That you want to enjoy every sunrise and every sunset because it means you have made it through another day without the darkness enveloping you. I see you longing for a time when you no longer remember what it felt like to be broken. That you want to meet new people and allow someone to love you again. I applaud you for visiting new places, for experiencing new things, and for embracing change. I know it is not easy to set yourself up for potential failure. I feel your nerves; I know they balance precariously between excitement and a fear so overwhelming that it threatens to make you flee to safety. The work you have put in to calm yourself and to build your self-esteem is awe-inspiring.

You are almost there. Happiness is within reach. It waits for you in the distance, and if you focus, you will be able to see it. It is not too far off. You will not have to struggle, or push through any more pain to get to it. You have pulled through the hardest part; the rest is a slow stroll while you readjust to the light. This part of the journey should not be rushed. Walk with me, and take in everything that the light touches; allow joy to fill you. Happiness does not happen overnight. It takes time, all miracles do; but you are getting closer every single day.

Don't let yourself be bogged down by life's hurdles; embrace every opportunity to feel happy. And take the time to look back at your progress too. You deserve to celebrate, and be celebrated.

Your biggest supporter.

THANK YOU

And here we come to the end of the road, stranger. Thank you for taking the time to read through my letters to you. I hope they helped you to look beyond your struggles and begin working on your recovery. You will find your strength; just take it one day at a time. I am so thankful for this opportunity to share my thoughts and feelings with you.

I hope that this book has helped you. And I hope you read it again in times of struggle when you need someone to give you the strength to carry on. I hope you choose to re-read these letters once a day, once a week, or once a month—as an opportunity to check in with yourself. Act on the advice I have given. Start a journal to allow yourself the time to reflect. Write down your thoughts and feelings; give yourself the opportunity to digest and organise them. You have the tools at your disposal now. Draw up a plan of attack and track your progress. Use apps, use the journal, and read my letters. There are so many options available to you. Make sure you take care of yourself. Take each day as it comes. Take each day as another opportunity to grow and learn and hope and love.

Hold on to my letters like a life guide that can offer support and understanding. But don't be selfish; share them with anyone you think might need to read them right now. With as many people who need them as you can. I hope they help.

Write your own letters, to yourself or to other people. Maybe write a letter back to me and tell me how you feel. I would love to find out how my letters made you feel.

Speak soon, dearest stranger.

even though it may seem like it
but i'm not writing about a broken heart,
i'm writing about a broken world
and the need to fix it.

ACKNOWLEDGEMENTS

Thank you Mom and Dad, for always loving me unconditionally and being so supportive. I owe you everything.

Thank you Savi, my beautiful wife and the best storyteller I know. You're the reason I write. This book would not have existed without you. So much love for you.

My friends and followers, for appreciating my writings and loving me for what I am. Thank you for always being there.

Thank you everyone at HarperCollins India, my publisher, for believing in me.

Forever grateful to the universe.

ABOUT THE AUTHOR

Ashish Bagrecha is a best-selling author and one of the most loved Instagram poets in India.

His books, *Dear Stranger, I Know How You* Feel and *Love, Hope and Magic* have sold lakhs of copies. He is a strong mental and emotional health advocate and voices his experiences and observations through poems and reels which have found a connection with millions of youngsters online.

Ashish is also a popular audio creator and you can listen to his podcasts and shows on Audible and Spotify.

You can know more about him on Instagram @ashish. bagrecha